HIS STORY

As Told By Himself

(Pertaining To His Younger Days)

A COMPILATION
FROM THE DIVINE DISCOURSES
OF
BHAGAWAN SRI SATHYA SAI BABA

PRASANTHI NILAYAM

SRI SATHYA SAI BOOKS & PUBLICATIONS TRUST
Prasanthi Nilayam – 515 134
Anantapur District, Andhra Pradesh, India
STD : 08555 ISD : 91 – 8555
Phone: 287375 Fax: 287236
email: enquiry@sssbpt.org

International Standard Book No. 81 - 7208 - 437 - 4

First Edition : **October, 2005**
Reprint : **December, 2005**
Reprint : **April, 2006**
Reprint : **January, 2007**
Reprint : **April, 2007**

Published by:
The Convener,
Sri Sathya Sai Books and Publications Trust
Prasanthi Nilayam, India - Pin Code 515 134.
STD: 08555 ISD: 91-8555
Phone: 287375 Fax: 287236
email: enquiry@sssbpt.org

Printed at:
Vipla Computer Services
(Designers & Multi Colour Offset Printers)
Nallakunta, Hyderabad - 500 044.
Ph. +91-40-27676910, 27654003
email: viplavision@rediffmail.com, viplavision@gmail.com

Publisher's Note

The Avatars have no duty to perform nor is there anything in all the three worlds that they are obliged to attain. Nevertheless, they are constantly engaged in the performance of *Karma* (action). In Dwapara Yuga, Lord Krishna Himself stood as an outstanding example of this truth.

Bhagawan Sri Sathya Sai Baba, the Avatar of the Age has led such an ideal and purposeful life, suffused with eternal values right from His childhood and stood as a beacon light for humanity. Ever since He was a young lad studying in the local elementary school, Bhagawan has been constantly striving to uplift the world. Every act of His was directed towards this noble goal. In His relation with His parents, relatives, elders in the village, classmates or His teachers, in fact, in every aspect of His life, Bhagawan set an example to others by living up to His declaration "My life is My message". In keeping with His *Avatharic* Mission to achieve die social, moral and spiritual development of humanity through the eternal values of *Sathya* (Truth), *Dharma* (Righteous

Conduct), *Santhi* (Peace), *Prema* (Love) and *Ahimsa* (Non-violence), He had undertaken several socially useful projects in the fields of Education, Medical Services, Drinking Water Supply, etc. Bhagawan Himself had narrated in some of His divine discourses a few incidents from His childhood which revealed His *Avatharic* Mission even at that tender age.

> "The great puppeteer called Paramatma
> conducts the cosmic play
> Keeping the embodied souls on the world stage
> Enjoy that Divine play, describing it a little",

said Bhagawan, on one occasion. Here is a compilation of some such incidents from His divine life as narrated by Himself in some of His discourses. We humbly offer this garland of anecdotes from Bhagawan's life pertaining to His younger days, at His Lotus Feet.

Prasanthi Nilayam
Dt. 21-09-2005

Convener
Sri Sathya Sai Books & Publications Trust

CONTENTS

1
God In Human Form

The Divine Child of Nanda has come again
As The Embodiment of Ananda to find His playmates;
The Lord Rama has come again
As The Blissful Ramachandra to find His subjects;
The Lord Easwara has come again
As Sai Easwara to play with His group;
The Lord Vishnu has come again
As The All–pervading Lord on this earth to collect
    His weapons;
That great Puppeteer called Paramatma
Keeps the Jivas on the stage of the World
And conducts the cosmic play;
Witnessing and describing a little,
Enjoy that eternal divine play.

(Telugu poem)

IN ancient India, the ladies used to perform the *Sathyanarayana Vratha* (a religious vow to propitiate Lord Sathyanarayana), with great faith and devotion. In keeping with that ancient tradition, the mother of this body, Easwaramma also used to worship Lord Sathyanarayana and listen to the divine story at the end of the ritual, in the company of Subbamma, her neighbour. On one particular occassion, it was very late in the afternoon by the time the *Vratha* was completed in the house of Subbamma. Easwaramma did not partake of her food till then nor did the other members of the family. All the members of the family were frustrated and resented the strict discipline accompanying the performance of the ritual, saying "why should there be so many rules governing the performance of this *Sathyanarayana Vratha*?" Easwaramma's husband, Pedda Venkama Raju denounced her insistence on the observance of these rules, strictly. But, Easwaramma was not yielding. She firmly and politely replied "you may take your food, if you are hungry. I am not hungry. I will take my food only after completion of the *vratha* and partaking of the *Sathyanarayana Prasadam* (sanctified offering made to Lord Sathyanarayana)". In the meanwhile, Subbamma had completed the *Vratha* and brought the *Prasadam* for Easwaramma to partake of the same. It is only after partaking of the *prasadam* that her pregnancy survived.

It is said *"Yad bhavam thad bhavathi"* (As you think, so will you become). The *Sthithi* (status) and *gathi* (destiny) of a human being will be in accordance with his thoughts and resolutions. Easwaramma was an illiterate. She did not learn even a single alphabet. Nevertheless, she used to have unflinching faith and devotion towards God. One day in the seventh month of her pregnancy, Subbamma came to her house and said "Easwaramma! your pregnancy survived only after you partook of the *Sathyanarayana Vratha Prasadam.* Hence, you name your child to be born as Sathyanarayana." The mother of Pedda Venkama Raju and mother–in–law of Easwaramma also agreed for this suggestion, with great faith and devotion to Lord Sathyanarayana.

A unique incident had happened before Easwaramma delivered a baby. Puttaparthi was a small hamlet tucked in a remote corner of Anathapur District, in those days. It had no modern conveniences like roads and water supply. There used to be a well in the midst of four houses, from which people used to draw water with the help of a small bucket, for their daily requirements. One day, Easwaramma was fetching water from that well. Suddenly, there was a flash of brilliant light in the sky. The wind blew and the cluster of divine light entered into the womb of Easwaramma. Subbamma, who just came out of her house, had also witnessed that scene. She told Easwaramma "I saw a brilliant light entering your womb." I did not reveal this fact to anybody so far. I am revealing this truth for the first time, so that people may realise that the nature of the Avathar will be so great and immaculate.

Pedda Venkama Raju was walking in front of the house of Subbamma, the previous day. Subbamma called him into her house and told him "Venkama Raju! you please name your son to be born as "Sathyanarayana." But, he did not give much thought to her suggestion, thinking that it was a foolish sentiment of the ladies. The next day, Easwaramma gave birth to a son at an auspicious moment early in the morning. It is natural for a child to cry, the moment it is born. But, this child did not cry. Observing this strange phenomenon, the ladies around got panicky that this child appeared to be a still – born child. Easwaramma too on hearing these words was very much afraid. She just pinched the child so that he may cry if he is not a still – born child. Instead, the child delighted the people around with an enchanting smile. What a great surprise! A new born child, not even an hour since he was born; he was displaying an enchanting smile! In the meanwhile, Karanam Subbamma arrived on the scene and told Easwaramma "I heard that you delivered a male child. I have come to see him." Subbamma was a Brahmin lady. The Brahmin ladies in those days were observing the orthodox customs and traditions very strictly. Hence, Easwaramma put her new – born baby on a cloth and kept him on the floor slightly at a distance. In the meanwhile, the mother–in–law came there and advised her "What Easwaramma! Subbamma came here with a lot of expectation to caress the child lovingly and you are keeping him at a distance! You put him in her hands." Easwaramma replied "Dear mother–in–law! I was afraid that she may be hesitant to touch a new born baby. That is why I kept him at a distance." In fact, Subbamma was not a lady to entertain such differences.

The boy was growing beautifully day by day, like the moon in the brighter fortnight of a month. However, his behaviour used to be rather strange. He was not talking to anybody. He was a *mithabhashi* (one of few words) and *mithahari* (moderate in in–take of food). The mother Easwaramma was surprised at his strange behaviour. Children usually will be craving for food. Whenever they come across an eatable, they stretch their hand. But, this particular child was not at all interested in food. Another characteristic of his was that he never used to allow non–vegetarian food to come anywhere near him. Also, he never used to visit the houses of non–vegetarians. Easwaramma could decipher from his behaviour that he shuns non–vegetarian food, since he was a divine child. The elder sister Venkamma was supporting her mother in all such matters. Both of them together were looking after this divine child very lovingly, constantly singing the glory of God. The child was growing in such a sacred environment.

2
The Philosopher

DURING My childhood, several children of My age used to gather round Me, singing and dancing and happily spending their time. I used to teach them a lot of things during that time. I used to tell them "Your mother undergoes a lot of suffering in bringing you up. She bears you in her womb for nine months and undergoes great physical suffering in giving birth to you. Your father also undergoes several difficulties in nourishing and nurturing you. Hence, you love your parents, first and foremost. Never deviate from the path of truth in your daily life, under any circumstances. Never speak untruth to cover up your faults, fearing punishment from your parents. It does not matter, even if they scold you or beat you; you always speak the truth. The power of truth is far superior to that of even an atom bomb. There is no greater and powerful missile than truth. Truth alone will protect you. Then, the question arises in what manner truth must be spoken. It is said *Anudwegakaram Vakyam Sathyam Priya Hitham Cha Yath.* "The truth you speak should not display any emotion. If you want to speak the truth, it need not be said loudly and emotionally. Truth must always be spoken softly, lovingly and pleasantly. The evil qualities like anger, hatred and jealousy must be given up." Normally, when children come across an article of their liking, they feel like grabbing it. Hence, I used to teach them "you should not covet others' property. Supposing you need a pen or a book, you take it from your classmates after obtaining their permission. Never take it without their knowledge".

There used to be a sizeable number of Muslims also in Puttaparthi. They used to celebrate the festival of Muslim Peers, in which the Hindus also used to participate. In that context, I used to teach the children "It is not the religion that is important. Morality is important. In fact, morality shall be the life–breath of a person. Hence, cast off all your differences of religion, and caste and be friendly with everyone. You also participate in the festival of Peers". While I was teaching thus, one boy got up and told Me "Raju! My parents will not agree for my participation in a Muslim festival. We are Brahmins." Then I explained "My dear! First and foremost, you are a human being. Your religion is love and your caste is the caste of humanity. Therefore, you always keep that principle of unity as your goal." The parents of these children were, however, not happy with My teaching. They thought that I was spoiling young minds by My teaching. They, therefore used to quarrel with Me saying, "What Raju! you are spoiling our children, teaching that there should not be differences on account of caste and religion." But, I was very firm and used to argue with them that there is no religion greater than love in this world. I was not afraid of any one. Why should I fear when I am speaking truth? We can achieve anything in this world, with truth as our weapon.

One day, all the children gathered and discussed among themselves "Raju is teaching us so many good things; but, are we able to implement even one among them?" Then, they introspected among themselves as to what extent each one of them had been able to put into practice My teachings. One boy stated "I am trying to speak truth under any circumstances." Another boy explained "I love God always. God is my mother, father and my very life–breath." His name was Kesanna. His mother was Buggapalle Acchamma. Poor woman, she used to earn her living by running a small pan shop selling cigarettes and beedies. Another boy agreed "it is not possible to implement all the good things taught by Raju. Nevertheless, I feel very happy to hear Raju explaining those things. In fact, his very words make everyone happy." Yet another boy stated "How can we be indifferent when Raju is teaching so sweetly and lovingly! I love Raju very much." In the end, all the children declared in one voice "Not only you, all of us love Raju very much." Thus, all the children around Me used to yearn for My love.

I used to gather the children and teach them a number of principles relating to spiritual *sadhana*. I used to teach them "Dear children! you must take only *sathwic* food. You should not eat meat or fish." In those days, several people in this village used to catch fish from the village tank and sell them for consumption by the villagers. That was their profession. I used to tell them that it is not proper to kill so many living beings for the sake of their livelihood and it is a sin to cause harm to the living beings. I also told them that they should desist from bad habits like smoking and drinking. It was customary in those days to organise bullockcart races. The villagers used to decorate their bullockcarts tastefully and yoke the bullocks to them. Ten to fifteen bulky people with large sized tummies used to sit in those carts and make the bullocks run faster and faster in the sand, by whipping them mercilessly. Unable to witness the great torture to which these dumb animals were put, I used to call the children one by one and tell them "Look! This particular cart belongs to your family. You tell your father not to beat those poor bullocks. You see to it that this does not happen again." Thus, I brought about a transformation in the elders through their own children.

Not only the bullockcart races, but competitions in cockfighting were also being held in those days in the villages. Knives were being tied to the legs of the cocks and they were encouraged to fight with each other. It was a fight to finish each other. I used to counsel with them "This is a most cruel and evil practice. Instead of arranging a competition in killing the dumb birds, why don't you organise a competition among yourselves to become a better person than the other?" Gradually, this matter has reached the father of this body, Venkama Raju. He called Me and chided Me "What! you are just a small kid. Why do you interfere in the affairs of the elders in the village? These are all unnecessary matters for you". I told him "I am not interfering in the affairs of the elders in the village. They are torturing mute animals and birds, just for the sake of fun. I do not at all agree for this." He realised that it is futile to argue with Me. He then instructed Griham Ammayi (Easwaramma) "at least, you tell him not to interfere in such matters." While serving food to Me, she tried to convince Me saying "Sathya! Why do you interfere in the matters pertaining to the elders? Your father does not like this. More over, you will get a bad name." However, I firmly replied to her, "I consider what I am doing as a good work. When I am thus engaged in good work, how can My name be ever tarnished?"

The grandfather of this body Kondama Raju then called the villagers and explained to them "Look! Our Sathyam is not doing anything bad. He is doing all good work only. You should not hurt any living being. You should not organise these bullock cart races and cockfights. They will, in the end, cause enmity between one another. Ultimately, peace and tranquility in the village gets disturbed." Thus, I could successfully prevent the bullockcart races and cockfights from being organised in Puttaparthi.

Every individual shall help his fellow human beings, to the extent possible. You must span out into the villages and slums in the towns and cities and help maintain clean and healthy environment. You must help the children by providing free food, clothing and education. If you can do this service, it will be of great help to the society. Not only now, even from My childhood, I am engaged in various service activities. I used to help others. Whenever a beggar stands in front of the house and asks for alms, the people in the house used to turn them away saying "go, go, not now." But, I used to bring food from the house without their knowledge and feed those beggars. If somebody wanted clothes, I used to give away My old clothes. I am telling you the truth. I had only one shirt and knicker per year in those days. I used to wear them at the time of going to the school and after coming home, I washed them daily, wrapping a towel around My body. After they are dried, I used to iron them with a brass jug–like vessel, putting live embers in it.

The Griham Abbayi (Pedda Venkama Raju) never used to scold Me or beat Me. He used to jocularly say "My dear! you are a great *thyagi* (renunciant). How can we rise to your level of detachment?" He used to call Me *"Vedanthi"* (The Philosopher). So also the Griham Ammayi (Easwaramma). She also used to treat Me with great love and care.

3

Kondama Raju, The Liberated Soul

THE grandfather of this body, Kondama Raju used to worship Venkavadhutha (a saintly person in the Rathnakaram lineage) regularly. He had two sons by name Pedda Venkama Raju and Chinna Venkama Raju. Pedda Venkama Raju was the father of this body. Kondama Raju's younger brother also had two sons, namely Subba Raju and Venkata Rama Raju. All these four sons were happily living together. Theirs was a conjoint family. However, the sons could live together happily as brothers; but not the daughters–in–law as sisters. In due course, there arose differences of opinion among the four brothers due to misunderstanding between the daughters–in–law. They, therefore, decided to live separately.

I was very young at that time. One day, Kondama

Raju during the course of a conversation requested Me "My dear! you have a pure and sacred heart. Whatever you speak is truth. I have made a resolve. I need your opinion on this." Then, I enquired from him, "Grandfather! What is that resolve?" He told Me "I want to separate these four sons." I concurred with his view saying "Very good! These four families lived together with tolerance and mutual understanding, all these years. Now, they have lost these values. Therefore, it is better to separate them. Kondama Raju then enquired "My dear! How do you know about this?" I replied "It is quite evident from their thoughts, words and deeds. What more proof is required?" Kondama Raju was very happy. He said "You have given a beautiful reply. I will put into action my plan today itself." He called the four sons and told them "My dear sons! From now on, you live separately and discharge your family responsibilities. Lead a happy life." They were also ready for this arrangement, since the ladies had lost their qualities of tolerance and understanding.

Kondama Raju called his four sons and told them "You share between yourselves all that belongs to our family. I don't want anything." Then, the sons pleaded with him "you please stay for a period of six months at each of our houses." Kondama Raju did not agree for this proposal. He told them frankly "I will not come to your houses. I don't need your food. Whatever I have

Sri Kondama Raju

Swamy with His grandfather

acquired, you share between you four, equally. But, give me one property which I value most". The sons enquired what it was. He told them "Give me Sathyam. If that one boy is with me, that would be enough. I don't need anything else." He asked me, "Will you come alongwith me?" I said, "yes" and went along with him. From then onwards, I used to stay with Kondama Raju.

Kondama Raju was very fond of Me. He had Divine Vision. He was a great devotee and a *Jnani* (Realised Soul). That is why, he had opted for Me. He had realised My divinity. He used to call Me "Sathya!" That *Sathya* (Truth) alone stood by him. My job in those days was to cook for him. He took a small room for rent. I used to get up early in the morning everyday and wash the utensils, cook food and thereafter run to attend to My School in Bukkapatnam. Puttaparthi did not have a middle school in those days. Hence, I had to go to the higher–elementary school in Bukkapatnam. Exactly at one o' clock, the bell used to ring signifying our lunch time. Then, I used to come running to Puttaparthi, serve food to the grandfather, eat some Myself and again return to Bukkapatnam, running all the way. That was My daily routine in those days.

Kondama Raju was, however, very sad that I was put to a lot of physical strain running between Puttaparthi and Bukkapatnam daily. He, therefore, advised "Sathya! you need not come all the way from

Bukkapatnam daily in the lunch hour, just to serve me food. I can serve myself. When you go to school in the morning, take some food alongwith you for yourself." In those days, it was very difficult to obtain even aluminium utensils in this remote village. Hence, I packed some semi - solid *ragi sankati* (gruel made of ragi cereals) in a cloth and took it to school for My lunch. As soon as the lunch bell rang, all the children gathered at one place to partake of their lunch brought from their houses. They brought some rice and chutney in small tiffin carriers. I had no rice in My cloth sack. Only *ragi sankati* was available. In fact, that was My staple food right from My childhood. I moved to a little distance away from those boys to take My lunch, lest they might think that I am a poor boy and cannot afford to eat rice. I was hesitant to partake lunch in their company with a feeling that I may be belittling the honour of our family. Everyone has to uphold the honour and dignity of his family, thus. The next day I approached Kondama Raju and informed him "Grand–father! If I take *ragi sankati* in front of all those boys, they may think otherwise. Hence, I will come home and take My food here itself, even if it is a bit difficult."

It might cause some physical strain for Me to come home for lunch from Bukkapatnam daily and again get back to that place, immediately after lunch. However, that was a better arrangement for Me. Pleasure is an interval between two pains. One cannot experience happiness without undergoing some difficulties. If an ornament is to be made out of gold, it has to be melted by putting it in fire; then it has to be hammered and cut into pieces. Thus, when gold is subjected to so many processes, it becomes a beautiful ornament. Hence, if one wants to enjoy happiness, one must undergo certain difficulties. I, therefore, informed Kondama Raju "Grandfather! I am prepared to undergo any ordeal. I don't shy away from difficulties. Infact, this is not an ordeal; it is a good exercise for Me." He was astonished at My reply and said "What sort of an exercise is this? Why such a big exercise at this tender age of eight years?" However, he could not say no to My decision. He loved Me intensely. He never used to believe any one, except Me. That is the reason why he attained such a noble end. Easwaramma used to visit Kondama Raju's residence every now and then and plead with him "Dear father-in-law! Please come and stay with us. You spend four months each at each of the houses of the four brothers. Don't we deserve to serve you?" He used to reply, "No; I have Sathya with Me. That is all right for me." He used to have such firm faith in Me.

I have not touched sweet ever since I was born. If I take sweet, hundreds of devotees will bring different varieties of sweets for Me. I don't ever take fruit or milk or curd. Mine is a simple food consisting of a small quantity of *sankati* (a semi-solid food made of *ragi* cereals), with groundnut chutney or a leafy vegetable. Kondama Raju also used to relish this food. He used to tell me, "My dear! whatever you eat, serve the same food to me also." As soon as I get up from bed, I used to finish off My daily chores quickly and cook some *sankati* and leafy vegetable or chutney for Myself and grandfather. All the people in our street used to like the food prepared by Me. By the time I returned from school in Bukkapatnam, all those who were suffering from fever used to wait in a line in front of our house. The moment I stepped into our house, Kondama Raju used to tell Me "My dear! These people are suffering from fever. It seems they desire to have the pepper *rasam* prepared by you. Please give them immediately." I used to quickly prepare that *rasam* and fill their tumblers with it. After partaking that pepper *rasam*, they used to feel relieved and happy, saying that their fever is gone! I am an expert in cooking. Hence, people in the neighbouring houses used to come to our house to take the curries prepared by Me.

There is a lot of difference between the old and new customs and traditions in the villages. In the olden days, the washerman and the barber used to come to the houses and take the food offered by the householders on festive occassions like Ugadi (Telugu New Years' Day) and Sankranthi. In our house, Myself and Kondama Raju were the only members. Hence, even on festive occassions, I

Myself used to cook for both of us and to others. During festive occassions, Easwaramma (the mother of this body) and Venkamma and Parvathamma (the sisters of this body) used to prepare *"Bobbatlu"* (a kind of sweet) in their houses. I thought why not I also prepare them in our house. Accordingly, I used to prepare *"Bobbatlu"* on such festivals and serve to the old man. I also used to feed the washerman and the barber sumptuously on these festivals.

On a certain festival day, while Myself and Kondama Raju were taking food, Pedda Venkama Raju (the father of this body) came there on some work. Kondama Raju invited him to partake food in our house saying, "My dear Son! Today is a festival day. You also take food here alongwith us." Venkama Raju agreed and had his food alongwith us. He praised Me saying that the items were very tasty. He made a comment also "I don't know what is wrong with these ladies. They don't take enough care to prepare the items tasty." He then went home and chided Easwaramma and Venkamma profusely. He also advised them, "Look! How tasty Sathyam is preparing the food and sweets like *Bobbatlu*! From tomorrow, you go to him and get me whatever items he prepares. I will eat only those items." Easwaramma and Venkamma were very unhappy at this unexpected reprimand. They came running to Me and ventilated their anger on Me saying "Sathya! Because of you, we had to face the wrath of father. Why do you prepare the food so tasty?"

One day, while I was sleeping during night, the sound of *omkara* was emerging from My breath. Kondama Raju, who was sleeping by My side, was surprised. He put his ear near My breath and heard the sound carefully. The next day early in the morning, he told Me "Sathya! My dear! We must celebrate this occasion." I enquired "Grandfather! What occassion?" He replied "The sound of *omkara* emerged from your breath last night." I tried to explain away the incident as a routine matter. I told him "Is this something new? It was always there." Thereafter, he used to hear the sound of "*Soham*", "*Soham*" now and then, while I was asleep. He used to come near Me and test whether I was breathing or not, putting his finger near My nose. He used to be surprised to hear the sound of "*Soham*" with no signs of breathing. Thus, Kondama Raju had several divine experiences.

One day, while I was cooking food, he closed the door, came near Me and called "Sathya! Sathya!" I enquired "What is the matter?" Thereupon, he held both My hands and pleaded "Sathya! These are not hands. I consider them to be your feet. I have a desire. At the time of my departure from this world, you must pour some water in my mouth with your divine hands." I promised him that I would do so. Thereafter, he lived for twenty years.

The name given to Easwaramma by her parents was Namagiramma. Having realised the Divinity in Me, Kondama Raju suggested to Pedda Venkama Raju to change her name as Easwaramma. Pedda Venkama Raju could not understand why he was making such a suggestion. Nevertheless, bowing to the wishes of his father, he gave her the name of Easwaramma. Kondama Raju thought that since she was the mother of Lord Easwara, the name of Easwaramma would be most appropriate to her. Once, he offered his *pranams* to her saying, "Easwaramma! you appear to be an ordinary woman. But, you are not! Lord Easwara Himself has taken birth in your womb. How fortunate you are, Oh! Mother!" In fact, she was his own daughter-in-law. Will there be a father-in-law or a mother-in-law who offer their *pranams* to their daughter-in-law? Kondama Raju gave a new definition to Easwaramma's name. He told her, "Easwaramma means the mother of Lord Easwara. Hence, your name has become sanctified and meaningful, Oh! Mother!" Another day, he called Venkamma and told her "I am sorry that all our people are leading a life of ignorance and innocence. No one seems to have recognised the divine power latent in Sathyam. This boy appears to be verily an Embodiment of Divinity. Neither He is hungry nor He feels the need for sleep. He is going without food, water and sleep for days on end, yet He is as fresh and active as ever." Thus, those who are able to realise the nature of

Divinity can rise to any level in comprehending Divinity. Those who are unable to do so can never realise Divinity, despite witnessing any number of divine *leelas*. How can the blind witness the brilliance of the Sun?

The glory of My Divinity was increasing day by day. Within no time, groups of people started visiting Kondama Raju's house. When someone questioned them why they were flocking to his house, they used to reply, "Kondama Raju has a grandson, in whom there is a lot of divine power. He appeared in our dreams and solved our problems." Time rolled on, thus. The elder brother of this body, Seshama Raju returned to Puttaparthi for vacation. He was under the mis-apprehension that the grandfather Kondama Raju was coming in My way to pursue higher education, keeping Me all along with him. He, therefore informed all the members of the family that he would take Me alongwith him to his place and put Me in the High School. He did not like several people visiting our house continuously, in search of Me. In those days, people used to hold the educated people in high esteem. Since Seshama Raju underwent Teacher Training course, he was considered to be a highly educated person and respected by the people. He came and argued with Kondama Raju "Grandfather! Don't allow anybody to visit this boy. This is not divine power or for that matter, any power at all! This looks like a kind of hysteria. Hence, ensure that no outsider visits our house."

4

Pandhari Bhajan

WHEN this body was passing through the age of 7 years, certain infectious diseases like cholera and plague were wide spread in the remote village of Puttaparthi. People were not sending their children out, out of fear that they might contract those diseases. There used to be strict instructions that no one should visit or partake of water in others' houses. The atmosphere in the villages was surcharged with mortal fear. These restrictions were being observed by one and all in the village including Griham Ammayi, Easwaramma. Kondama Raju was a very orthodox person. He never took even water in anybody's house. He confined Me to the house and never used to allow anyone to come near Me, lest I might contract those infectious diseases. He used to be so strict that he did not allow even Venkamma and Parvathamma (elder sisters of Swami) to come near Me. However, I used to go out every now and then, without his knowledge. Later, when he came to know about it, he used to plead with Me lovingly, "you should not go out like that, Sathya!" The house in which we were living was located in a street where *Boyas* (the hunting community) were residing. Kondama Raju, therefore, put some *Boyas* as My "bodyguards." He used to tell them "Keep a watch on the movements of this boy. If you find him anywhere in the village in the company of others, bring him home immediately". Thus, he made strict arrangements restricting My movements. But, do I submit Myself to such restrictions? I used to stealthily go out, without being noticed by anybody. Some boys, however, out of love for Me used to come to our house without the knowledge of their parents. They were all aged between 6 to 8 years. A group of ten to twelve boys used to gather round Me. They used to move alongwith Me constantly, wherever I went.

One day, the children came running to Me out of fear and pleaded with Me "Raju! we understand cholera is rampant in our village. We also understand that it is a deadly disease and a person infected with this disease will die within a short time. We don't know what will happen to us. We are very much afraid." Then, I assured them that nothing will happen. I tried to instill courage and confidence in them saying, "you don't be afraid. The body is bound to perish, however much we try to protect it. Growth and decline are bound to occur in the life of a human being, even if one were to live in a forest. Hence, you don't be afraid of death. However, you make efforts to keep the disease away. For that purpose, engage yourself in the constant contemplation on God." The children then enquired from Me, "Which God? Rama or Krishna?" They were very innocent boys. Puttaparthi was a small hamlet in those days. It had a population of only 106 people, then. I suggested to the boys that we would conduct *Bhajan* in the village at six o' clock in the evening by installing an oil lamp in a prominent place. They were in a dilemma as to which *bhajan* was to be sung. Then I composed some devotional songs. I told them "Dear children! We need not search for God outside. He is very much immanent in us." The children went round the entire village singing *bhajans*, as instructed by Me. In those days, people in the village used to be very much afraid of ghosts. Hence, they dare not go beyond the Sathyabhama Temple after five o' clock in the evening. They thought that that was the boundary for the village. However, I tried to infuse courage and confidence in the children, explaining that there are, infact, no ghosts or devils at all! I could make the children bubbling with enthusiasm to drive away the diseases of cholera and plague from the village, with faith in God and constant contemplation on Him. I told them to tie jingle bells to their ankles. I put castanets in their hands. With this paraphernalia, we walked upto the river chitravathi singing *bhajans* all the way. By the time we covered the entire village and its boundaries in three days singing *bhajans* thus, the diseases of cholera and plague disappeared forever.

Thereafter, the parents of these children came to Me and requested "Raju! you instilled courage and confidence in our children and made them very enthusiastic. You be a Teacher to our children from tomorrow, you teach them whatever you know. No other education is necessary for them." From that day onwards, all the children started coming to our house for tuition. I was being addressed as "Tuition Master". One day, the parents of the children came to Me and requested Me to receive *Guru dakshina* (some kind of remuneration as a token of gratitude to the Teacher). How much of it? A quarter of an anna per month. The children used to come for tuition in the evening after partaking some *sankati* (ragi gruel) and stay with Me for the night. I used to teach them some spiritual and moral topics also, alongwith the alphabets. I used to tell them "You should not move in the company of bad people. You should not lend your ears to what they say. You should not speak bad words. You should also not criticise others. You must cultivate good qualities. You should respect your parents and elders. You should not harm anybody. You should not hurt others' feelings. We must do our work properly. Besides, we must undertake social service. Whatever good things we learn, we must teach them to others." In due course, a change for the better was achieved in the children by such good words. In addition, I used to train some younger children in *bhajan* singing and conduct *Pandhari bhajans* with their participation. These young boys used to tie jingle bells to their ankles, hold castanets in their hands and go round the village singing *bhajans* during early morning and wake up those who were still sleeping. In those days, the villagers used to sleep till 7 o' clock in the morning. But, once I started *Pandhari bhajans* with the help of these young children, they used to get up at 5 o' clock itself, take bath and offer their prayers to God in that serene and holy atmosphere. In fact, it was only due to the efforts of Sri Sathya Sai Baba that contemplation on God had started for the first time in Puttaparthi. Gradually, it spread to the other villages also. Due to such transformation brought about by My teachings, all the villagers used to address Me as "*Vedanthi*" (The Philosopher).

The children used to go round the village every day early in the morning and exhort the villagers by singing such songs as:

"Wearing the ochre robes;
Holding the cymbals in hands;

Girding up the loins;
Destroying desire and anger and
Treading the path to Divinity;
Come! Come! Oh! Villagers! Come quickly;
Join us singing hail to Lord Panduranga!"

That was, infact, the *Nagar Sankirthan* we conducted in the village in those days. And, when was it started? When this body was barely 7 years old! While we were thus singing and dancing and going round the village early in the morning waking up the villagers from slumber, Subbamma and Easwaramma used to experience bliss. Subbamma too used to participate in that *Pandhari bhajan* clapping her hands rhythmically. In those days, a bag of puffed rice was available for one anna. She used to purchase one bag and distribute to the children some quantity as *prasadam*. Thus, I used to spend My time in the propagation and teaching of spiritual matters right from My childhood. People from nearby villages also used to visit Puttaparthi to witness these *Pandhari bhajans* and get totally immersed in them. The reason why I am relating all these stories is that students should cultivate divine feelings right from their childhood.

5

On The Sands Of The Chitravathi River

THE month of *Magha* had commenced. I told the children "The holy bath taken in the month of *Magha* is very sacred. However, it is not enough if you simply perform this *Maghasnana.* You must also undertake circum-ambulation in a temple." Accordingly Myself and the group of children around Me used to visit the Anjaneya Temple as early as 4 o' clock in the morning. There used to be a big lake behind the Anjaneya Swami Temple. We used to take our early morning bath in that lake. However, the small children could not get up from bed so early. Hence, I used to lift them up, take them to the lake and bathe them, personally. After taking bath, we used to go to the temple. Once, all of us went to the temple. I told the children, "You perform circumambulation to Anjaneya Swami and come back. I will stay here". They went accordingly. However, they discussed among themselves, "Why not Raju also come along with us? He taught us so many things. Without Him, we cannot undertake any work. Hence, He should lead us and we must follow." Having made such a resolve, they came running to Me and said "Raju! you must accompany us." I told them, "I will come. But first you go and finish your circumambulation and come." However, they were very insistent that I should accompany them. They firmly told Me, "unless you come, we will not go." I told them "I have pain in My legs." They then informed Me "We will lift you and carry you physically." Thus, when they were pressurizing Me so lovingly, I could not say no. I, therefore, started doing circumambulation to the Anjaneya Temple, alongwith them. Believe it or not! A big monkey suddenly appeared from nowhere and stood in front of Me, obstructing My way. The children around Me wondered "We did not see such a big monkey in this village, so far! From where did it come!" They tried their best to drive it away; but it did not move. Who is that monkey! It was Hanuman, the servant of Lord Rama, verily! They did not realise this Truth. Hanuman himself had come in the form of that monkey and prayed "Swami! I am the one who had to do circumambulation to you. You should not do it for me." Accordingly, I

Anjaneya Swami Temple

The Idol of Anjaneya in the sanctum sanctorum.

On the sands of the Chitravathi river

informed the children "Hanuman did not like My circumambulation to him. Hence, I will give it up." From that day onwards, a lot of transformation had taken place in the children. They experienced divine feelings. While returning home, they informed everybody: "Today, when Raju was performing circumambulation in the Hanuman Temple alongwith us, a big monkey appeared from nowhere and stood in front of Him, preventing him from doing circumambulation." During the full-moon nights, we used to go to the Chitravathi river. All of us children used to spend time happily on the Chitravathi sands right from 6 o' clock in the evening till late in the night. The elders also used to join us. They used to play Kabaddi and some other games. I used to encourage the children "you also go and play. If the body is to be healthy, there must be sufficient exercise for it." But, the children were reluctant to leave Me. They used to insist "Raju! we are interested only in *bhajans*. If you sing, we will follow you." Sometimes, they used to request Me to compose new songs. I used to compose a number of songs. They used to be surprised of My poetic skills saying, "Raju! How did you acquire these poetic skills?" They used to sing the songs composed by Me and feel very happy. They used to praise Me very much saying, "Raju! You compose beautiful songs and set them to good tunes." I used to tell them, "If you have any wishes to be fulfilled, tell Me. But don't praise

Me like this."

In those days, several children used to follow Me, for example Kesanna, Ranganna, Subbanna, Ramanna etc. Those children were very dear to Me. They also used to love Me very much. Their Love and innocence cannot be described in words. A boy of seven years used to place My head on his lap and put Me to sleep saying "Raju! you are very much tired. Take rest for some time." After some time, he used to say "Raju! since you had placed your head on my thigh and slept, all the pain that was there earlier had disappeared. I experienced some inexplicable joy". Thereafter, the other children also used to crave for that privilege. They chalked out a method by which all the children would get such an opportunity. According to that, I was expected to place My head on each one's thigh and relax to a count of 50 numbers each time. Thus, I used to provide joy to one and all.

There used to be an elderly gentleman of 70 years in those days in that village. He used to walk upto the Sathyabhama Temple, then wash his feet and sit on the pial, relaxing. One day, while I was walking in front of him, he called Me saying "Raju! come, come!" I went near him and enquired what he wanted. He replied "Raju! I am bulky. I have a plumpy thigh. Please sit on my thigh for sometime." I enquired what benefit he would derive by My sitting on his thigh. He replied "I cannot describe that benefit in words. It is infinite and miraculous. Not only that, Raju! you are like a brilliant light for Puttaparthi. In the years to come, your name and fame will spread to the entire world."

His word has come true in letter and spirit. The name and fame of Raju as well as that of Puttaparthi have spread far and wide not only in the country of Bharat, but to the entire world. In those days, it was very difficult to reach Puttaparthi, even by walk. Such a remote village of Puttaparthi has earned a prominent place in the world map now. Subbarayudu, of course, forecast this metamorphosis even in those days. Poor man! He had no children. He hugged Me very affectionately and said "Raju! How fortunate I am to have taken you on my lap and made you sit there for sometime. A time will come when the entire world will crave for your benevolent look even for a fraction of a second. He also told Me "myself and your father are not on talking terms with each other. Your father does not like me to talk to you even. Hence, please do not reveal to him, what had transpired between us". I, however, replied "There is nothing wrong. I will tell him the truth. He is a good man."

As soon as I returned to the house, Griham Abbayi questioned Me "Why do you talk to that Subbarayudu?" I enquired, "Why I should not talk to him?" He replied "He is my enemy." I told him "May be he is an enemy to you, but not to Me. Hence, I talked to him. I see nothing wrong in it." Then, with folded hands I requested him "Look! you are an elderly person. You should not hate anybody. Remove hatred and develop our village with unity among all the villagers." Then, he enquired "What is that Subbarayudu talking to you?" I replied "He is stating that on account of My divinity this village of Puttaparthi will shine as a beacon light to the entire world." On hearing this reply, Griham Abbayi became very angry. Seething with anger, he questioned "What is that divinity in you that these people extoll so much?" Then I brought some flowers. Holding them with both My hands, I threw them on the ground, saying "Do you know who I am?" Miraculously, the flowers arranged themselves as "Sri Sathya Sai Baba" in Telugu letters. From that moment onwards, Griham Abbayi conducted himself very carefully in his relations with Me. Thus, I used to teach good things to both children as well as elders, right from My childhood.

6
Education In Bukkapatnam

TODAY, I am revealing certain incidents that had happened during My school days in Bukkapatnam. I would also like to tell you in this context as to what sort of relations should exist between the students and what rules and regulations they should observe in their student career. Puttaparthi was a remote village in those days with no modern facilities and conveniences. You already know about it! This body did not visit any other village in those days, leaving Puttaparthi. However, the body used to visit Bukkapatnam daily to attend to the school. Myself and some other children used to go to the Bukkapatnam school, together. The family in which this body took birth was very poor, then. The other children in the village were also very poor. The Griham Ammayi used to prepare some *sankati* (ragi porridge) for My lunch. That was My semi - solid staple food. She used to make a small hole in the centre of that *sankati* and put some groundnut chutney in it. There were no tiffin carriers in those days. I used to pack My lunch in an old cloth and hang it on my shoulders, while going to the school. The lunch bell used to be rung at one o' clock in the afternoon, daily. As soon as the bell was rung, we used to run upto the village tank. But, I could not eat My lunch immediately, since the *sankati* was dried up and stuck to the cloth. Hence, I used to go to the tank and hold the lunch packet soaked in the water for a few minutes. Then, the solid stuff comes out of the cloth. Among our classmates, there used to be a boy who belonged to a rich family. He used to get rice mixed with soup. He used to share it in small quantities with all the children. I also used to share My *sankati* with all the children. Thus, we used to experience the joy of sharing in our food and recreation. There is so much joy in unity. Unfortunately today, the spirit of unity and love are extinct in the educated class. Instead, jealousy and hatred are increasing day-by-day.

I have to tell you about a small matter in this context. The Teachers in the school used to love Me very much. Every Teacher, as soon as he entered into our class room used to enquire "Did Raju come?" Do you know how I used to be in those days? I was not

Bukkapatnam School

Sri Mehboob Khan

having dozens of pants and shirts, like the present day students. I used to have only one pair - one knicker and one shirt for the entire year. As soon as I returned from school, I used to wrap a towel around My body and wash the knicker and shirt and keep it ready for the next day. Thus, I used to manage with only one pair of clothes for the entire year. I used to answer well, all the questions put to Me by the Teachers. But, the other boys were not able to do so. The literacy rate in the British times was very low. There used to be boys who were quite old in age, even in the Vth class. Infact, I was the only student, who was the youngest of all students.

We used to have an English Teacher, by name Mehboob Khan. He had immense love towards Me. And, that love was born out of *Atmic* relationship, not bodily relationship. He used to be very eager to take up our class. The moment he entered the class room, he used to pressurise the teacher, who till then was teaching, to leave the class immediately, whoever he may be. As soon as he sat on the chair, he used to call Me and make Me sit by his side. He used to put his hand endearingly on My shoulders and stroke My head lovingly. He was fifty years' old then. He had no children. Hence, he used to invite Me to his house, frequently. He was a great devotee. The moment he entered our class, all the children used to make fun of Me, saying, "Ah! Raju! go, go near his chair!" That was an embarrassing situation for Me. If I obliged the Teacher, the children used to make fun of Me. If I don't go to the Teacher as ordered by him, I don't know what he will think of Me! Nevertheless, I did not inform the Teacher that the boys were making fun of Me. Neither did I ever behave arrogantly with the children, simply because the Teachers were treating Me so affectionately. One day I approached My Teacher and explained the position in a firm, but soft tone, thus: "Sir! If you call Me only out of all the boys, they may think otherwise. Please do not, therefore, call Me to your side. Allow Me to sit alongwith those boys." The Teacher, however, got angry at My pleading. He told Me frankly "Let them think what they wish to. I am not bothered. I am not doing anything wrong. Therefore, I do not fear anybody. In fact, I am loving all the children. But, I love you, a little more. This is due to the divinity latent in you." Whenever any savouries like Pakodas are prepared in his house, he used to bring some for Me, packed in a newspaper. I used to humbly reject them saying "Sir! I do not know whether some non vegetarian dishes were cooked in your house. Hence, I am sorry, I cannot touch these pakodas." The Teacher then used to assure Me and plead with Me "No, Raju! I am telling you the truth. I swear on Myself. I don't at all allow such things to happen. I have brought these eatables with great love and affection towards you." After obtaining such an assurance, if I would take a small piece of that item and eat it, he used to feel extremely happy and grateful, shedding tears of joy.

There used to be a Teacher called Iyengar in our school. The students in those days used to have respect as well as fear for this Teacher. If they happened to see Sri Iyengar anywhere in the market place, the children used to silently slip away into the side lanes, out of fear for him. Sri Iyengar came to know of this practice. One day, he was under the misapprehension that I too was avoiding him like the other children.

I used to be the Monitor for our class. I am so "big" even now. You can imagine how short I was in those days. It was My duty to bring one long twig of a tamarind tree and keep it ready in a corner of the class room before our Teacher Sri Iyengar entered our class, daily. One day, he took the twig into his hands as soon as he entered the class and demanded "Hey! Raju! come here". I went near him boldly, since I was sure that I did not commit any mistake. He enquired "Why did you slip into the side lane the other day on seeing me?" I answered very coolly. "Sir! I did not see you. My note book is with that boy who lives in that lane. I went into his house to take back My note book." I spoke the truth. Thereupon, he shouted at Me "Did you not see me, really?" I replied that it was a fact that I did not see him. Then he threatened Me that he would beat Me. I replied,

"As you please". At last, he realised that I was speaking the Truth. He called Me to his side and said "Raju! I know you are not like the other children. But, I was under the impression that you are committing a mistake, though you are not in the habit of committing a mistake. That is why I am angry. I am sure you won't commit a mistake. You please drop into our house once tomorrow, on your way back to your house".

His house was on the way to our house. The next day I went to his house, as per his command. I stood in the verandah, thinking that I should not enter the house of the Teacher, without his permission.

Our Teacher had already given instructions to his wife, "A boy by name Raju would come to our house. When he comes, you bring him in". Accordingly, she came to Me and enquired "My dear son! Are you Raju?" I said "Yes, Mother!" "Then, you come in; your sir is calling you", she said. I went inside the house. His love for Me, knew no bounds. He brought two pakodas in an aluminium plate and put it in front of Me and said "Raju! I am sorry I wanted to punish you, for no fault of yours. I realised my mistake. In order to correct that mistake, I would like to make friendship with you." See! How our good nature, good qualities, purity and truthful words can move and melt even a stone-hearted person! I humbly replied "Sir! I am a young boy of about 7 years. You are an elderly gentleman and moreover our Teacher.

What is your level and status and what is mine? How can you make friendship with Me?" Then, he tried to convince me saying "My dear son! you don't entertain such differences. It is not the age or education that are important; it is the purity of the heart that is important. You are a very good boy. That is why I would like to make friendship with you." So saying, he enquired whether I was studying well. I said "yes". Then, he advised Me, "You are having examinations during next month, study well."

Our examinations commenced as per schedule. We were given two hours to answer the question paper in each subject. But, I could finish writing My answers within half-an-hour. I placed My answer sheet on the table of the examiner. He was a bit surprised and enquired, "Raju! you don't seem to have answered the questions well!" I answered "Sir! I have written all the answers correctly. You yourself can see it tomorrow." The next day he took out My answer sheet from the bunch and went through it. He could find therein, some topics, about which he himself was not aware. Then, he wrote on My answer sheet "Very very very very good." In those days, our Teachers used to keep all our answer sheets with them only. The next day, he invited Me to his house for coffee. He said "You please take a cup of coffee in our house and go." I politely rejected his offer saying "Sir! I am not in the habit of taking coffee or tea.

Then he requested Me, "you please take atleast one dosa." I humbly replied, "I don't take anything at this hour." Thereupon, he pleaded with Me "My dear son! You please take something, atleast for my satisfaction." I could not refuse. I took a dosa, to please him. The students shall thus please their teachers. Some students are very much afraid of their teachers. But, I was never afraid of our teachers. Why should I be afraid, when I did not commit a mistake?

The students and teachers must love each other. The students can win the heart of their teachers with love, however tough the teachers may be. Similarly, the teachers can also mend the students with love. It is only when we love others that others also would love us. The teachers should understand the love and behaviour of the students, well. There should be cordial relationship between the teachers and the students, based upon love and understanding. The most essential message of the Indian culture and spirituality is "*Sathyam Vada, Dharmam chara*" (speak truth and practise righteousness). This message has to be translated into action, by one and all. In those days, the teachers could understand My nature well. On My part, I also used to be very humble, respecting the teachers and elders. Same is My message to the students, even now. "You cannot always oblige, but you can always speak obligingly." Sweet and soft words can melt the heart of any one.

However, we are obliged to speak harshly on certain occassions. I can be harder than the diamond, when occassion demands. But, I can also be softer than butter, in matters of love.

In those days, after we returned from our school in Bukkapatnam, Easwaramma used to make all the children sit around her and enquire "My dear children! what had happened in the school today?" One day, in answer to her query, one boy informed her "Mother! Today, one of our teachers made Raju stand up on the bench". So saying, all the children started criticising the teacher. Easwaramma could not bear this criticism against a teacher. She counselled the students saying "My dear children! you should not say anything against your teacher. He must have punished our Sathyam thus, only when he had committed a mistake. No teacher would ever punish his student, without a reason." So saying, she enquired from Me "Sathya! what mistake you have committed, tell me." Then I narrated the incident exactly as it had happened, thus:

The teacher ordered "Whoever had written the notes dictated by me in their note books put it on my table; others may stand up on the bench." Since I did not write the notes, I stood on the bench. However, I explained to the teacher "Sir! No doubt I did not write the notes dictated by you, but I can answer all the questions put by you." The teacher felt offended by My reply. Expressing his annoyance, he said "How arrogant you are?" and ordered Me to stand up on the bench for three periods consecutively. In the meanwhile, our English teacher Mehboob Khan came that way. He was a noble soul. On seeing Me standing upon the bench, he enquired that teacher "Why did you make him stand on the bench?" He replied that this boy did not write the notes. Mehboob Khan explained "It might be true; but He can answer any question you put to Him. Hence, tell Him to sit down on the bench. What you did is a mistake." Despite Mehboob Khan's advice, the teacher Kondappa did not agree to the suggestion. In the meanwhile, the bell rang signifying the end of this period. The teacher tried to get up from his chair so that he may go to another class. But, he could not get up. He looked around to see whether his dhoti got stuck to some nail. There was no such thing. What had happened was that he himself got stuck to his chair and hence could not get up. Mehboob khan, on seeing the plight of this teacher told him again 'We should never punish people without a reason, even if they are our students. This boy may appear to you as an ordinary boy. But, there is immense divine power in Him. You ask Him to sit down, at least now'. Kondappa then ordered Me to sit down. The moment I sat down, the teacher Kondappa could get up from his chair".

While the teachers were thus treating Me with great

love and affection some of the boys were jealous and started developing hatred towards Me. They, therefore, used to push Me and drag Me in the Chitravathi sand holding My legs, during our return trip to Puttaparthi from the school. They used to splash dirt on My clothes and tear off My shirt. But, I used to keep My cool, inspite of whatever they did to Me. I used to tell them, "Love is My form; tolerance is My nature. You may do whatever you like." So saying, I used to walk up to the tank near the Anjaneya Swamy Temple and clean my clothes there with water.

In those days, I was not having even a safety pin to put together a torn shirt. That was our condition. There was no money in the house. Nor I was prepared to borrow from someone. That was My firm resolve. There used to be a cactus plant near the Sathyabhama Temple. I used to pluck a small thorn from that plant and used to join the torn parts of the shirt with that thorn. Such was My firm resolve to uphold the honour and dignity of the family. One can achieve anything in life if one is wedded to the Truth and makes such a firm resolve. From that day onwards till today, it has been My vow not to accept anything from others. Subbamma was, however, anxious that I was becoming thinner and thinner day by day and therefore used to advise Me "Raju! How come, you are becoming weak? In this young age, you must eat well and grow strong." My friends also used to bring whatever was prepared in their houses and try to pressurise Me to eat that stuff. But, I used to tell them sternly not to bring any eatables from their houses for Me. I used to firmly reject those items saying, "You eat meat in your houses. Your people cook fish curry in your houses. Hence, please do not bring any eatables prepared in your houses, for Me."

In the meanwhile, our public examinations were fast approaching. They were to be held in Penugonda, a nearby Taluk headquarters . In those days, people were so much afraid of going from Bukkapatnam to Penugonda, as if they were going to Russia or America. There were no buses even to go to Bukkapatnam, in those days. There was not even a "pucca" road. It was for the first time that a rail line was laid to Penugonda and a train service was introduced. The villagers used to weave fantastic stories about the train, saying "It seems that the train comes like a gigantic caterpillar with one eye." The train was a eighth wonder to the villagers in those days. They used to go to Penugonda in large numbers making use of the bullock carts, just to have a look at this strange object. Such being the condition of the village and the people inhabiting them in the days, I had to go all the way from Puttaparthi to Penugonda, to write My public examination. Hence, the mother of this body, Easwaramma prepared a variety of eatables for Me to partake during My journey. She was very much worried that I was going to some distant foreign country. She, therefore, packed these items in a piece of cloth and gave it to Me. There were no tiffin carriers in those days, as we have now. When this body started proceeding to Penugonda, Venkamma and Parvathamma (the sisters of this body) and all other friends and relatives could not control their emotions and started crying. They all came alongwith Me upto Bukkapatnam. From there, eight of us students hired a bullock cart to go to Penugonda. One of our Teachers accompanied us. The roads were so bad then that if we travelled a distance of one mile in the bullock cart, we had to get down and walk for five miles continuously. Since the entire terrain was full of ups and downs, we had to get down from the cart, whenever there was a steep gradient. Thus, we underwent a lot of difficulty getting down from and getting into the bullock cart. My problem was compounded by My short stature. Even now I am short. You can imagine how 'tall' I was in those days. I felt it would have been better if we went by walking all the way. Further, there were other children in the bullock cart, who were younger to Me. Hence, Poor man! it was our Teacher who had to bear all the strain of bringing down and putting them back into the bullock cart all through the journey. The Teachers in those days had great love and affection for the students. We started from Bukkapatnam as early as 5 o'clock in the morning and reached Penugonda as late as 9 o' clock in the night. There were no hotels or lodges for us to stay, in those days. Same is the position in the Bus stand and the Railway station. There was, however, one choultry on the outskirts of the town, where we settled down. We took some rice, cereals and other essential items alongwith us, while starting from Puttaparthi. Besides, some mirchi powder and chutney powder was also available with us. I used to cook rice for all of us. We used to take some rice alongwith the chutney. Thus, we spent three days in Penugonda. I am not revealing this information out of ego or for earning a name, but it is a fact that among all the students who wrote the examination it is only Swami who passed the examination with Ist class. All others failed in the examination. After we returned to Bukkapatnam, the people of that town extended a warm welcome to Me and took Me through the streets in a big procession, since I was the only student in the entire Taluka (Revenue area) who passed the examination, that too in first class. There was no further scope for Me to pursue higher education in Bukkapatnam. Hence, Seshama Raju (the elder brother of this body) took Me to Kamalapuram, his in-laws' place, for higher education.

One day, while I was returning from Bukkapatnam, a mother was sitting at a particular place chewing pan, combing the hair of her daughter for lice.

She did not notice My coming that way. She suddenly spat, which fell on My shirt. I cannot describe in words the embarassment she felt on noticing that her spit fell on Me and spoiled My shirt. Immediately. She brought a towel from inside her house, wrapped it around Me, removed My shirt and washed it clean then and there. Such was the love and affection shown by the villagers in those days. They were such noble and simple folk that they remember till their end, any help that they might have received from others. The reason why I am narrating this incident is to stress the point that purity and gratitude are very important qualities for a human being. Infact, ingratitude cannot be atoned for. Hence, you must be grateful till your end to those people from whom you received help of any kind. During My childhood, people 20 to 30 years older to Me even used to approach Me with a request to teach them alphabets. They used to make a living by raising flower gardens and selling the flowers. As soon as I came home, I used to teach them alphabets. Hence, they used to respect Me very much saying" Raju is our *Guru* (Teacher)". When they came to know that I will be leaving for Kamalapuram shortly, they were very much disappointed. They brought one paisa each as *Guru Dakshina* (a token of gratitude to the Teacher). I told them "Why are you offering Me this money? Keep it with you." But, they insisted on My accepting this token of their love and gratitude towards Me. Their *Guru Dakshina* added up to twelve paisa. They followed Me by walk upto Bukkapatnam. They repeatedly enquired from Me "Raju! when will you return to our village?" Such was the love and affection of the villagers in those days. But, today the situation is totally in contrast to that. The humanness has declined an account of modern education. The sense of gratitude has become extinct. That is the reason why the country is facing several difficulties to day. The most important quality of a human being is gratitude. The villagers of those days used to conduct themselves with a great sense of gratitude, respect and courtesy.

7
Education In Kamalapuram

KAMALAPURAM was a small town near Cuddapah, a district headquarters in the state of Andhra Pradesh. Seshama Raju, the brother of this body took Me there and admitted Me in the Middle School. There used to be acute water scarcity in that town. As soon as I get up early in the morning, I had to walk long distance and bring water from a canal in a big earthen pot. The process had to be repeated both morning and evening, daily. With the result, I had practically no time to read My lessons. By the time I completed the job of fetching water from the canal in the morning, it used to be 9 o' clock already. Immediately, I used to partake of some *ambali* and rush to the school. *Ambali* is a sort of diluted *ragi sankati* that was left over the previous night, to which a little salt will be added for taste. In those days, there were no tiffins like iddly, dosa, vada, upma etc., or potato kurmas for breakfast. It was the practice in most houses to partake of some rice that was left over the previous night, mixed with a small quantity of pickle. There used to be wooden desks in our class for the children to sit. They were prepared in such a model that the students can keep their books underneath a plank and write their notes etc. with the support of the plank above. They can also sit comfortably on the bench attached to the desk. Three of us used to sit on one such desk. In our desk, I used to sit in the middle and two boys named Ramesh and Suresh on either side of Me. Ramesh was the son of a Sirasthaḍar (a revenue official of the State Government). Only the three of us used to get first class in every examination.

A village fair used to be held on a big scale every year in a place called Pushpagiri which was located in between Kamalapuram and Cuddapah. The Drill Teacher in our school who was also the Scout Master, insisted that all the children must compulsorily participate in the scout camp and help the people visiting the fair. He also instructed that all of us shall provide ourselves with a pair of khaki shirt and knicker, alongwith a leather belt and a whistle. He told us that all the children should be ready with the scout uniform in a week's time. He issued an order that all the children shall go to Pushpagiri and serve as scout volunteers in the fair being held there.

How can I procure all these items? I don't have even a paisa in My pocket. Neither I can approach My parents for this purpose, since they themselves were short of money then. In those days, a person having a ten rupee note in his pocket was considered to be a wealthy person. If one had a hundred rupee note, he was verily a millionaire!

The father of this body gave Me two annas, at the time of My coming over to Kamalapuram to join the school here. In those days, two annas was a big money. It had great value. Since My father belonged to a poor family, he could give Me only two annas. I could manage the last six months of My stay here, with those two annas. I had absolutely no money left with Me. I was the monitor of My class, then. Hence, as a matter of convention I had also to be the leader of our scout group. Following this convention, the Drill Master ordered Me to lead the scout camp at Pushpagiri, without fail. He told Me "you must be ready by such and such date. You must bring these children, fully prepared." My problem was "how can I attend the scout camp without the uniform? " I thought over the matter deeply. Infact, I used to have only one pair of clothes - a shirt and a knicker, for the entire year. As soon as I come home, I used to wrap a towel round My body and wash My school dress clean. I had no money to get the dress ironed by a dhobi (washerman). Hence, I used to put some live embers in a small brass vessel and iron the clothes. Thereafter, I used to keep them under a trunk for pressing. The next day I used to wear those pressed clothes and go to the school. Thus, after continuous "Wash and wear", the clothes were worn out and gave way here and there. I did not have money even to buy a safety pin. I used to join the torn parts with a cactus thorn. Since I was thus managing with one shirt and knicker for the entire year, how can I afford to purchase a new pair of khaki shirt and knicker for this scout camp? I could not also say that I will not attend the camp. Moreover, it will be damaging for the honour and prestige of the family to admit that we cannot afford to purchase a khaki dress for the scout camp. I was in a real dilemma as to what to do in the circumstances. I thought over the matter carefully and devised a plan to tide over the situation. I informed My classmates "I am not feeling well. Hence, I cannot attend the scout camp." I took care, however, not to reveal this ploy to the Teacher. I selected a boy among the students to be My assistant and told him "you lead these boys to the scout camp. I will come later". But, the children refused to attend the camp in My absence. They protested in one voice "Raju! If you are not attending the camp, we will also stay back." Not only that, they even came to our house and started pressurising Me to lead them to the scout camp. They did not leave Me alone even in the classroom. It had come to a stage where I was unable to withstand their pressure. My classmate and benchmate Ramesh who was the son of a Sirasthadar could understand My predicament well. He was of the same size as I was. He went to his father and requested him "Father! I like the khaki dress very much. Please get two pairs of khaki shirt and knicker sticthed for me." His intention in asking for two pairs was to give Me one. He was really fortunate in entertaining such noble ideas of helping his friend and classmate. Such type of *samskara* (noble thoughts) comes to a person from previous births. Ramesh, however, did not reveal his plan either to Me or his father. Since he was the only son to his father and his father was a well-to-do person, he got two pairs stitched as per his request. Ramesh then got one pair of khaki shirt and knicker packed in a newspaper and put it in My desk alongwith a small chit. He wrote in the chit "Raju! I am like your younger brother. If you do not accept this dress, I will commit suicide by throwing myself under a moving train. Please therefore, accept this dress without-fail." I noticed this packet and chit in My desk. I took out the chit and tore it into pieces. I wrote another chit. "It is true that you are like My brother. However, the friendship between us cannot last longer if it is based on a 'give and take' relationship. Such type of relationship cannot be a permanent one. Ours is a 'heart-to-heart' and 'love for love' relationship. If you really wish that our friendship shall last forever, you should not do such things. If friendship between two individuals is to develop, only love is to be exchanged between them, not articles. If articles are exchanged, love ceases to exist. Hence, if you wish that the friendship between us shall not be affected, you take away this dress." Ramesh felt very sorry on reading My letter. However, he could not disregard My feelings. He, therefore, took back the dress. The children in those days never used to disobey My command.

Several boys keep their study tables very unorganised, with the books strewn all over. They make it clumsy and dirty. But, I used to keep My books always neat and tidy. In those days, very few boys were in a position to purchase new books when they were promoted to a higher class. Every four or five years, the text books were being changed. I always used to keep My books neat, like new books. Hence, boys studing in the lower standard who were promoted to the higher standard, used to take My books. During a particular year, a poor boy approached Me and requested for My books. I showed all My text books to him. In those days, there used to be high syllabus even for lower classes, in subjects like History, Geography, Civics etc. On seeing My books, he commented "Raju! you don't seem to have touched your books at all! They appear to be brand new.' I told him "My habits and behaviour keep them like new books." The cost of My books totalled to twelve rupees. But the poor boy was not in a position to pay even that much. Then I told him "My dear! I am selected by our Teacher for the scout camp. I have to purchase khaki dress and shoes. Besides, there are other items of expenditure. I don't have money to incur that expenditure. Nor I would like to ask My parents. What I need at the moment is five rupees. Therefore, pay Me five rupees and take away these books". The boy felt very happy and immediately paid the amount. In those days, currency notes were very rare. Therefore, he paid the entire amount in small coins, packed in a piece of cloth. It was tied in an old cloth, which gave way unable to bear the weight of the coins. The coins were strewn all over the room, making a big sound. On hearing the sound, the lady of the house came there and enquired "Where did you get all this money? Did you steal from my trunk?" So saying, she slapped Me. The poor boy witnessing this incident explained to her "Mother! I gave those coins to Raju towards the cost of his books, which I purchased from him." She did not believe his words and took away all the money.

The next day, all My classmates were going to Pushpagiri where a cattle fair was being held to participate in a scout camp. I told My Teacher that I would start the next morning and join the group. Early in the morning, I set out on My journey by walk. I walked a long distance and before I could join My collagues, they had left for their breakfast. As for Myself, I did not have even a paisa in My pocket. What do I eat for My breakfast? I thought I would manage somehow without eating anything. I purposely avoided My classmates then, lest they might enquire whether I had breakfast. My classmates were, however, searching for Me, making enquiries, "Did Raju come?"

There was a masonry tank nearby in which water was stored for bathing the cows and buffaloes. The water was very dirty. But, what can I do? In those circumstances, that dirty water itself is *ganga*! I was feeling very tired, hungry and thirsty, having walked all the way. I, therefore, washed My face with that dirty water and drank some. Then I noticed that someone had left behind a packet of beedies (country cigarette) and a one anna coin on the tank there. The beedies were, of course, of no use to Me. Therefore, I threw them away. I took the one anna coin and exchanged it for four smaller coins (*botlu* or *kanis*). As I was returning, I noticed a person sitting on the roadside playing cards spread over a cloth and inviting passersby to bet on a particular card. He invited Me saying "Raju! you are a very lucky boy. Come! come and bet some amount on any card you like." He offered double the amount to the winner. No doubt, this was a sort of gambling, but I was completely helpless at that time. I, therefore, put one coin each on different

Swami as a boy scout in Pushpagiri

The cattle fair in Pushpagiri

cards. Everytime I was winning the bet and getting double the amount I invested. Thus, I played the game till I could make sixteen annas (one rupee). Then I thought that that was the end of the game and returned with the money already earned. Since I was feeling hungry, I purchased three *dosas* with one *bottu*. In those days, *dosas* were available at the rate of one for a *dammidi* (1/3rd of a *bottu*). Thus, I managed with two bottus a day eating *dosas*. I joined the scout duty alongwith My friends. During night, I kept the bundle of coins under my head and slept on the sandy floor. Since I was very much tired due to long walk, I was lost in sound sleep. During sleep, my head slid to a side and the coins bundle came into the open. Someone noticed that bundle and took it away without disturbing Me. When I woke up the next day, I noticed that the cloth bundle containing money was stolen by somebody. I had no money to buy even one *dosa*. My classmates were very much dejected at My plight. They were infact, crying. They pleaded with Me to eat atleast one *dosa*, which they offered to buy for Me. But, I flatly refused. I told them I was not hungry, since I did not like to avail Myself of others' help. Especially, I did not wish to touch others' money. So saying, I left that place.

After conclusion of our scout camp, I purchased some sweets, fruits and things like that for taking home. As soon as I stepped into the house, I noticed that Seshama Raju was drawing lines in a note book, with the help of a ruler. He was very angry that his wife had to fetch water during my absence for 3 days and she was very much tired. I offered her the fruits and sweets brought by Me from Pushpagiri. Instead of accepting them gracefully she threw them away saying "who wants these things?" Seshama Raju was infuriated, after this incident. He took the ruler into his hands and beat Me on the forearm. The ruler broke into three pieces. My hand was swollen. I was helpless. I could not also reveal this incident to anybody. I tied a bandage Myself with a wet cloth to the swollen hand. The next day, one of the sons of Seshama Raju died. He gave a telegram to Venkama Raju in Puttaparthi. In those days, there was no Post office or Telegraph office in Puttaparthi. The telegrams were being sent to Bukkapatnam and from there, a messenger used to take it to Puttaparthi. Pedda Venkama Raju used to go to Bukkapatnam regularly to purchase some items in the village fair. He saw that telegram there and immediately rushed to Kamalapuram. By the time he reached Seshama Raju's house, all the members of the family were immersed in sorrow. I too had to pretend to be sorrowful, since I am beyond joy and sorrow! In the meanwhile, Griham Abbayi saw My hand tied with a bandage and enquired how did it happen. I tried to explain away very casually as if nothing had happened. I told him that a small boil had appeared on the forearm and it was giving Me pain and therefore I put the bandage. Pedda Venkama Raju was, however, not convinced with My reply. There used to be a lady belonging to the Vysya community by name Subbamma in the neighbouring house, who used to make her living by preparing and selling *dosas*. One day, she called Griham Abbayi and told him "What! Venkama Raju! I know you are sufficiently well-off so as to get Raju educated at your place. Why should you put Him to so much trouble by keeping him under the care of his elder brother at such a distant place? You do not know how much suffering the boy is undergoing here. He has to fetch drinking water from a distant place carrying two big pitchers with the help of a *kavadi* on his shoulders, daily. He is put to a great ordeal here." In the meanwhile, it was night fall. Griham Abbayi expressed a desire to go out for answering his nature's call. There was no light in that place. I held a small kerosene lamp in one hand and a jug of water in the other. After reaching the outskirts of the town, Griham Abbayi asked Me "Sathya! stop! stop! put the lamp on the ground." He held both My hands and cried profusely. He told Me "My dear son! one can make a living even by selling salt, if only one is alive. Did I send you here, unable to bring you up? Why are you undergoing so much suffering here? I being your father, never beat you even once till now. These people are putting you to great ordeal. You start immediately and come along with Me." I tried to pacify him saying "No, No. What these people say is not true. No one here is putting Me to any trouble." He was not convinced and insisted on My going back to Puttaparthi. Then I explained the situation carefully thus: "It is not proper for you to take Me away from this place right now. If I go away from the house now, there will be no one to attend to the work in the house. You don't think otherwise. You please go now and I will follow you later." I did not make a complaint against the family members here. I never revealed the fact that My hand was swollen only on account of Seshama Raju's beating Me. I never had the habit of complaining against elders. I always tried to protect the dignity and honour of the family.

I tried to convince Griham Abbayi saying "It is not proper on My part to inconvenience these people, especially when they were immersed in sorrow due to the passing away of their child. Not only that. The neighbours may also think bad of Me, if I come away with you in the present circumstances. We must also be mindful of what others may say about us. We, should, therefore not give any scope for such things. You please go to Puttaparthi now. I will come after a fortnight, if you wish." On hearing My reply, Griham Abbayi shed tears. He left for Puttaparthi alone, saying "My dear Son! How noble are your qualities! It is only your good nature that will protect you." Before leaving, he enquired, "Do you need any clothes?" I replied, "I have plenty. I don't need anything." He felt very happy and left. However, before leaving he contacted a shopkeeper by name Kotte Subbanna and told him "If our boy approaches you for any help, please oblige. If he needs some clothes, please get them stitched and give him. You don't worry about the money. I will send you." As soon as he reached Puttaparthi, he wrote several letters one after the other asking Me to start immediately. He also wrote in some letters "your mother is serious, start immediately", since he was doubtful of My coming there. I knew that there was nothing serious, so far as her health condition was concerned. Hence, I stayed in Kamalapuram itself with Seshama Raju till the examinations were over. In the meanwhile, things came to normal with the passage of time.

Wolf Messing

During My student days in Kamalapuram, Myself and a few other students used to go to the Railway Station every evening regularly for a walk. There we used to spend sometime discussing spiritual topics. In those days, there were not many trains touching Kamalapuram. One or two trains in a day used to pass through that Railway Station. Oneday we were sitting on a bench in the Railway Station. The boys were asking some questions and I was answering them. In the meanwhile, a white - skinned foreigner by name Wolf Messing saw Me through the window of the train approaching the station. He tried to get down from the train even before it stopped. He fell down. My classmates Ramesh and Suresh who were sitting with Me were anxious "Oh! God! Poor fellow! He might have broken his leg." I firmly told them "Nothing has happened. He is coming to see Me only. Hence, no danger will happen to him. You remain clam and quiet."

He did not have even a hand bag, in his hands. He

was shedding tears of joy, gazing at Me. Ramesh and Suresh witnessed this scene. In those days, the children were very much afraid that the white-skinned foreigners would take boys forcibly and join them in the Armed Forces. Hence, Ramesh started running to his house on seeing Messing approaching Me, with the intention of informing the position to his parents. As soon as he reached home, he informed his father "Father! some foreigner had alighted from the train just now to take away our Raju. You must start immediately in a Jeep." He rushed to the Railway Station, lifted Me up, put Me in the Jeep and drove Me to his house saying "Raju! I will take you to your house after sometime. Let us first go to my house." Wolf Messing followed the Jeep. He sat before that house for a long time. Whenever he could see Me through the window, he used to wish Me and try to communicate something to Me. But, the members of the house closed all doors and windows, forbidding any sort of communication between us. Seshama Raju (the elder brother of Swami) was working as a Teacher then, in the same town. The father of Ramesh sent a word to him through an attender thus: "One white-skinned foreigner is waiting outside our house with an intention to take away Raju, forcibly. Raju is presently kept in our house only. I will bring him and drop him in your house safely, after sometime." Thereafter, Wolf Messing returned to the Railway Station, boarded some train and left for somewhere. Before he left, he wrote on the front door of the house with a pencil "you are most fortunate to keep

The Board Middle School in Kamalapuram

Sri Kotte Subbanna

Kamalapuram Railway Station

Wolf Messing

this boy who is an Embodiment of Divinity in your house and serve Him. I am not that fortunate. I deserve only this much. Thanks." Thereafter, he left for Russia.

Wolf Messing came to India after a long gap of several years. He went to Kamalapuram and enquired about Me. By then, I was no longer the same "Raju". My name had changed. The local people informed Messing "He had now become a *Guru*. His name is Sri Sathya Sai Baba. He may now be available either in Puttaparthi or Bangalore." He came to My *Asram* in Whitefiled, Bangalore. On that day, several devotees were sitting there, waiting for someone. When he made enquiries, he was informed that they were waiting for "Sri Sathya Sai Baba's *Darshan*." He also waited. While I was moving in the *Darshan* lines, he thought to himself: "This is the same person whom I saw way back in Kamalapuram. The same divine effulgence is shining brilliantly here also." Thereafter, he met the principal of the Brindavan College, Narendra. Narendra was a great Teacher, who used to teach the students well. His father's name was Damodar Rao. He was working as a Judge. Narendra's father-in-law's name was Sunder Rao, who was an eminent doctor. Both of them were there at that time. Messing commented in their presence "Swami is verily God Himself. He is at present not manifesting Himself in his true form. You are able to see his normal human form only. If you can visualise the Aura round Swami, you will realise his true nature". The next day early in the morning while I was giving *Darshan* to the devotees who assembled there after completing the *Nagar Sankirthan*, Wolf Messing could visualise great effulgence round My body. Later when he met Me, he shed tears saying "My dear ! you are my everything. I am your instrument. You are my everything." I have shown him what all is to be shown to him. I told him what all is to be told to him. I also explained to him "Inaccordance with the saying *'Daivam Manusha Rupena'* God incarnates in human form and appears as an ordinary human being." Later, He returned to his native country, Russia. After a few days, Principal Narandra received a letter. Messing wrote in that letter "How fortunate you are to work in an Educational Institution established by God, Himself. I wish that you please write letters now and then informing me of Swamy's Divine *leelas* and *Avatharic* Mission." One day, Myself and Narendra were sitting together and discussing something. Suddenly Messing appeared there from nowhere. How did he come there? Nobody knew. He had no ticket to come to India. He just came, saw Me and disappeared as quickly as he came there. That was a great miracle that not all people could witness. Neither all can understand the phenomenon, even if I try to explain.

8

The Poet of Poets

I used to write beautiful poetry in those days. Even now I can make use of chaste language in My discourses, but I am restraining Myself to a certain extent, lest the translator may find it difficult to translate My language. One day, a Provision shop owner by name Kotte Subbanna who used to sell some popular Ayurvedic medicines also, came to Puttaparthi on some work. He came to know that I write beautiful poetry. Hence, he wanted to get some songs written by Me for the propagation of the medicines sold in his shop. He enquired in the village about Me. "I understand that there is a young boy in this village, by name Raju. It seems he writes beautiful poetry. Where does he live?" All people directed him to Subbamma's house. He approached Subbamma and enquired "Mother! Do you know anything about that boy Raju?" She gave a very good account of Me saying "Dear Son! I know him very well. He is a boy of good qualities, good habits and good behaviour. He teaches good things to people." On that day, she invited him for lunch in her house. During lunch, he sat alongside Me. He was not very much impressed by My stature. He was not convinced of My capacity to write good poetry. He confessed "Raju! you seem to be very young. How can you undertake propaganda for my medicines? I am doubtful." I replied "If you are doubtful of My talents, you need not come to Me. Please leave Me alone. You can go to some one in whom you have confidence and get your work done." So saying, I sent him away.

Later, when I was sent to Kamalapuram for higher education, he approached Me again saying "Raju! I heard that you write very good poetry. Look! If you can write a good piece of poetry for me, I will get a pair of shirt and knicker stitched for you. I told him bluntly "Do not speak such words. Am I waiting for your charity? If you put forward such proposals, I will not talk to you even." Then, he apologised to Me. I also yielded a bit and told him "Subbanna! I have nothing to do with the business of give and take. Hence, keep your business tactics aside. You tell Me the name of your medicine, its salient features and its efficacy. I will compose an appropriate song for that medicine." He stated that a new Ayurvedic medicine by name "Bala Bhaskara" has been received in his shop and requested Me to compose a song for propagating that medicine. He also explained what are the different kinds of diseases which the medicine can cure and said "I will gather a few children who can learn that song and go about in the villages singing that song. That will be a good advertisement for the medicine." Accordingly I composed the following song:

"There it is! There it is! Oh! children
Come! Come!
There is the medicine Bala Bhaskara;
Be it an upset stomach or a swollen leg;
Be it a joint pain or flatulence;
Be it any ailment, known or unknown;
Take this Bala Bhaskara for an instant cure!
If you wish to know where it is available,
There is the shop of Kotte Subbanna;
It is in that shop you can pick it up.
Come here boys! come here
It is an excellent tonic
Prepared by the famous physician
Gopalacharya himself,
come here boys! come here."

(Telugu Song)

When he heard this song, Subbanna was lost in joy completely. He ran to his house immediately and brought a basketful of laddus and tried to offer me. But,

I politely refused them saying "Don't bring them to Me. You distribute all of them to the boys." I don't touch sweats at all! Ever since My birth, I never touched a sweet. I have plenty of sweetness in Myself. My mind is sweet, My speech is sweet and My love is sweet. Then, where is the necessity for all these sweets? I distributed all the sweets brought by Subbanna, to the children. Thus, eversince My childhood I have been helping everybody and providing joy and happiness to one and all. In fact, that has been My main task. Kotte Subbanna made the young boys sing this song in every street and every village nearby. Thus, vigorous propaganda was conducted, due to which the entire stock of 'Bala Bhaskara' in his shop was sold out in no time. He was extremely happy. He brought two pairs of shirt and knicker for Me to express his happiness and gratitude, which I flatly refused saying "Subbanna! Are you giving these clothes to Me in return for the song I wrote for you? The Lord who receives offerings from the devotees (Lord Venkateswara) is in Tirupathi. I am not that Lord. I don't accept the articles brought by you." He felt very unhappy and said that he will not take them back to his house. Thereupon, I told him "O.k. That is good. Then give them to the beggars outside." Thus, My nature has always been to give to others, not to take from others. My hand always gives to others, does not accept anything from others. But, I am stretching My hand and asking you for only one thing, that is pure and unsullied love. Even that love is not your property. That is the property of God. Hence, I am asking for My own property. You are, at present, misusing this invaluable property of love. You are expending this sacred and invaluable property in sundry pursuits. That is why, you are encountering sorrow. When you dedicate this pure and unsullied love to God, you will be the happiest person in this world.

Once the stock of Ayurvedic medicine Bala Bhaskara was completely sold out and Subbanna received good profit, the other shopkeepers came to know about it and started making a bee line to Me with requests to compose songs for propagation of the products stocked in their shops. I obliged two or three shopkeepers by writing songs for their products. In the meanwhile, Seshama Raju came to know about it. He grew angry and chided Me saying "Since there is vacation for the school now, you go away to Puttaparthi. You are indulging in unnecessary activities, remaining here. Don't stay here." He sent Me back to Puttaparthi. As per his instructions, I returned to Puttaparthi. But, I did not stop writing poetry.

One day, some boys came to Me and requested "Sathya! we are putting up a playlet. You please write the story, dialogues and songs for that playlet and help us." Then, I told them "O.k! you give Me two boys." I composed some songs and taught them to those boys. In those days, the ladies started putting a small dot of *kumkum* on their forehead instead of a big one as per the normal practice and also started wearing thin gold chains instead of a necklace of gold coins. On observing such odd fashions, I composed the following song:

"How times have changed, my dear boys!
How times have changed....
Face powder has made its appearance and
Turmeric has disappeared
How times have changed, my dear boys!
How times have changed...
Necklaces of gold coins have disappeared and
Gold Chains came instead
How times have changed, My dear boys!
How times have changed...

The wrist watches made their entry then, for the first time. The *Karanam* (Headman) of the village used to tie one wrist watch to his left hand and wear costly *dhoties* and go about displaying vanity. If any one wore a wrist watch in those days, he was considered to be a great man. Deriding such vain-glorious practices, I wrote the following song:

People wear some glittering white badge to the left hand
With leather belt tied to it.
What fashion is this, Oh! Dear;

What fashion is this?
Disgusting appearances they are;
What fashion is this?
Long mustache is trimmed and shaved;
Few hairs are kept under the nose, instead;
What fashion is this, Oh! Dear!
What fashion is this?

In those days, people used to wear small insect like mustache under their nose. They are called Hitler mustache. It was considered to be a fashion in those days. When the boys sang this song for two days consecutively the Karanam shaved off his mustache immediately. Thus, I started reforming the elders in the village. I used to observe their weaknesses, compose appropriate songs deriding their behaviour and make the young boys sing those satirical compositions in front of their houses. I tried to bring certain transformation in them. Some of them, however did not take them sportively and attempted to beat the children. Then, the children used to tell My name, as the person who trained them to sing such songs. All of them used to come to our house and complain against Me, to the Griham Abbayi. the Griham Abbayi never beat me or scolded me. He did beat all other children in the house, for example, Janakiramaiah, Kistappa, Venkamma and Parvathamma, but not Me. He used to counsel Me endearingly "My dear son! why should we have to take the affairs of all the people in the village, on our head? You please don't write those songs." I, however, used to pretend as if I knew nothing about it, saying "I don't know who wrote those songs. I am innocent." I used to write such songs and dramas and teach the children good things with a view to dissuade them from being enamoured of fashions and inculcate in them our ancient noble ideas.

Once Subbamma came to Me and expressed her anguish that her husband was taking to bad ways and getting spoiled. She asked Me "Raju! you are teaching so many good things to so many people. My husband is taking to bad ways. Why don't you try to correct him? I told her "I will certainly correct him and bring him back to senses. I will compose some songs using strong words and make the children sing them in front of your house. But, you should not feel bad about it." She was afraid that he may get angry. I assured her "Don't worry! One's anger is one's own enemy. I will not be affected by his anger." Subbamma's husband used to sit near the Tulasi Brindavan in front of his house, every day evening. I composed a song, set it to good tune and taught the same to a group of children. I told them to sing that song in chorus in front of Karanam's house. The children were afraid that he may take them to task for their audacity. I, however, assured them "I will be behind you, protecting you always. You don't be afraid." The name of the

Karanam was Narayana Rao. He took to bad ways. He cannot be corrected by soft words. It is only by making use of strong language against him that he can be corrected. Hence, I composed the following song and prompted the children to sing the song in front of his house.

"Don't seek the company of women of loose character;
Surely you will fall down.
Your caste people will not allow you into their homes;
Your relatives will neck you out, if they see you;
Your friends will beat you with chappals,
If they see you in the company of such women."

I wrote the song with such strong words and indirectly warned him to stop his nonsense. When the children were going on the street and singing this song particularly in front of his house, the Karanam grew very angry. He immediately got up and went inside the house. Thereafter, he sent word through a servant to the children to see him. The children were very much afraid that he may punish them severely. He asked them "who wrote this song for you?" They replied "Raju wrote this poem and asked us to sing in your presence." He also knew that it was My handiwork and none else can dare do it. He called Me the next day and handed over plenty of mango fruits and requested "Raju! Please do not teach such songs to the children." Thereupon, I requested him "Karanam Sir! you are an elderly person. You also promise that you will not indulge in such activities." He promised that he will not do such things hereafter. I reciprocated his gesture with a promise that I will also not embarass him by writing such songs.

Subbamma came to know of this incident. She felt very happy. While I was going that side, she came running and fell at My feet, poor lady! She complimented Me for My courage, saying "Sathya! you are certainly not an ordinary child. Your physical stature is small, but there is infinite power in you. I have not come across anyone who can oppose the misdeeds of elders with such courage and forthrightness. Later, she told Griham Abbayi "Venkappa! you are deluding yourself by considering your son as an ordinary school - going lad. This boy has immense potential in him. In course of time, he will set an ideal for the entire world. Don't fall a prey to the *Maya* (illusion) under the influence of filial love. You send him to My house." Griham Abbayi replied firmly "I don't like to give away My son in adoption to others. I will bring up My child with whatever I have. I don't send him to others' houses." Thus, I used to bring about transformation in the elders, though I was a child Myself. I used to spend a free and uninhibited life, with courage and confidence; for, I had no faults in Me. Why should one have fear, when he is faultless? I have no fear at all! I used to move forward with courage and confidence.

In those days, Kameswari the mother of Panchangam Ramappa used to gather some elderly ladies round her and teach spiritual matters. I also used to attend those sessions. She used to read a number of books on philosophy. Though she was not able to understand the intricacies of the subjects contained therein, she used to explain to those ladies to the extent she could understand. She was no doubt making a sincere effort, poor lady! For example she used to discuss in those classes, such intricate spiritual topics as the following:

"Without coming under the veil of forgetfulness,
Always in the waking, dream and deep-sleep states,
One should constantly be aware of
The Soham manthra that would enable
you to realise the Atma Thatwa.
By the grace of Sadguru,
Oh! Man! cultivate the sense of discrimination".

(Telugu poem)

She used to make an effort to teach such highly philosophical subjects to totally illiterate women. In those days, very few women had education. Hence, they used to attend the *sathsanga* conducted by such learned elders. I was waiting for an opportunity to approach the elderly lady conducting that *sathsanga*. One day I was able to contact her. I requested her with all humility and respect "Dear grandmother! How can those poor illiterate ladies understand such highly philosophical concepts couched in such high language? It would be better if you can kindly explain to them in a simple language that they can understand, giving out the meanings of those technical terms." With a view to inculcate a spiritual bent of mind in the village folk, I established such forum even at that time. I have been explaining the significance and impact of the *sathsanga* to the people, since then.

Once, a political leader by name Narayana Reddy came to Me from Bukkapatnam and requested, "My dear! I understand that you write good poetry. If you can write some good poems on our National heros, we will publish them in the Newspapers." That day, they organised a political meeting. I composed the following poem and sang it on the stage, placing a rubber doll in a cradle and rocking it gently:

Do not cry, my child, do not cry.
If you cry, you will not be called a valiant son of Bharat.
Go to sleep, my child, go to sleep.
Did you get scared because the terrible Hitler has invaded the invincible Russia?
Go to sleep, my child, go to sleep.
Do not cry, my child, do not cry.
For the Red Army is marching under Stalin.

They will put an end to Hitler.
All the countrymen shall unite and fight to win freedom;
Go to sleep, my child, go to sleep.

(Telugu Song)

Thus, I composed a song picturising a scene as if an infant was crying and the mother was consoling him with an assurance that everything will be alright and there is nothing to worry about the fate of the country. I sang this song in an inspiring tone for about half-an-hour, keeping in view the freedom fighters. All the audience were happy and their joy knew no bounds. They wondered "How could this young boy know about Hitler, Stalin and Russian heros? These are all foreign names which none of these people, even elders do not know." Some police people (Britishers) also attended that meeting. When I was singing this song, they heard it with rapt attention. They could not, however, understand the meaning of the song. It was a song composed in the Telugu language. Nevertheless, they enjoyed the song appreciating Me "This boy is singing well. He is a small kid." When all the audience in the meeting clapped their hands, they also did it. The meeting thus ended most successfully. Thereafter, this song was printed in a pamphlet and distributed to the people in all the villages. The organisers of the meeting brought me gifts of shirts, knickers and towels as a token of their appreciation and gratitude. But, I distributed those items to the children around, even before their eyes. I told them "I did not write this song anticipating these gifts in return. I wrote it only to inspire you." I sent them away. Thereafter, several leaders of other political parties approached Me for writing songs about the activities undertaken by their parties. I told them frankly, "There will be misunderstandings between the parties on account of My writing such songs. I am sorry, I cannot write any more songs for political parties. In fact, I have nothing to do with any political party. All parties are Mine! All people are Mine! I belong to everyone!"

By now, people started coming to Me in groups and groups. In the meanwhile, Seshama Raju had returned to Puttaparthi for vacation. He was also a Poet. He was undergoing teacher training then. He observed that everyone in Puttaparthi was discussing about the poetic talents of the young Raju. He became jealous of Me, once again. He thought "This boy should not be allowed to continue here", and took Me away to Uravakonda, a nearby town, alongwith him, to admit Me in the High School there.

9

School Day In Uravakonda

IN those days, Sri Lakshmipathi was the Headmaster of the High School in Uravakonda, a nearby town to Puttaparthi. As soon as he entered the school, he used to call Me to his office. After My going into his office, he used to close the door, make Me sit in his chair and massage My feet, sitting on the floor. I used to plead with him pretending innocence "Sir! you should not do like this." But, poor gentleman! He used to reply "You do not know. But, I know. There is great divine power in you." It is not possible for every one to develop such noble feelings. It is only by accumulated merit from the previous births that such noble feelings develop in people. Our English Teacher in Bukkapatnam, Sri Mahboob Khan was also transferred to Uravakonda. There used to be good

Teachers in the Uravakonda High School in those days. One such Teacher was Sri Perraju. Sri Tammiraju was our Telugu Teacher. All these Teachers had great love and affection towards Swami. In those days, they were not much aware of Swami's divinity, but due to their accumulated merit over their previous births they used to raise their hands and offer salutations to Me even without their knowledge, the moment they saw Me. But, they used to withdraw their hands, the moment they realised that it was after all their own student. I always used to teach My fellow students in the school good things like "Do not abuse any one; respect elders."

Once, the School Day was to be celebrated during a particular year. In that context, the teachers came to Me and requested "Raju! you have a melodious tone. You can sing well. You please sing some songs on the school day." They also pressurised Me to put up a drama on the occassion. In deference to their wishes, I wrote a drama entitled "Cheppinatlu chesthara?" ("Will you act according to your words?") and acted in the main role. You might be aware of Smt. Kadapa Rama Subbamma. She was the first lady to become a District Board President in those days. She was invited to the prize distribution ceremony to give away the prizes to the winners. The entry to that day's programme was by tickets. This idea was conceived to help mobilise funds for the school building. The organisers of the function

Uravakonda High School

Smt. Kadapa Ramasubbamma

Sri Thammi Raju

H.S. Venkataramana, Lakshmipathi and Perraju
(from left to right)

put up an advertisement in the newspapers that Rishyendramani, a famous dancer of the times would give a performance on the occassion. But, unfortunately she could not make it to the programme for some reason. In the meanwhile, Lakshmipathi, the Headmaster was in great tension, for, he invited the District Collector to preside over the function. In those days, the Collector was greatly respected, like the governor of a state. Similarly, the people used to fear the police very much, in those days. The situation then was like that. The Head Master was undergoing great tension thinking, 'Oh! The Collector had come. The District Board President had also come. But, there is no trace at all of Rishyendramani, the dancer!" I observed the situation and went near him slowly and requested him in a pleasing voice "Sir! If you don't mistake Me, I have a proposal for your consideration. I will Myself perform that dance item to be performed by Rishyendramani. You don't get upset, Relax." The particular dance item Rishyendramani used to perform was like this. She used to keep a bottle over her head and a plate thereon in which some wick lamps are kept burning. With this load on her head, she used to dance. As a climax to her dance programme, she used to lie down on the floor and lift a handkerchief kept there, with her teeth. During the entire programme of her dance, no disturbance is caused to either the bottle or the wick lamps in the plate kept thereon, over her head. This particular dance item was the chief attraction of her dance performance. I told the Headmaster that while Rishyendramani can lift only the handkerchief on the ground with her teeth, I would lift a needle kept on the ground with my eye-lids. I also told him, "You may give an announcement accordingly; but tell them that Rishyendramani herself had come and is giving this performance." So saying, I started preparing for giving the dance performance. The make-up man brought a big silk Sari and wrapped it round Me. My hair was arranged with a long plait and decorated with ornaments that are to be worn by a traditional dancer. The jingle bells were tied to My legs. The make-up man ensured that all this decoration remained in-tact during My dance performance. They, then made Me seated in a rickety old car and brought Me to the venue of the dance programme. People came in large numbers purchasing tickets, thinking that Rishyendramani herself had come. The programme commenced. I came on the stage, for giving performance. Some of the audience started alerting their friends in the side seats, who were dozing. Wherever you see, the name of Rishyendramani was on the lips of every body. When Rishyendramani's name was actually announced, I made a pleasant sound with the ankle bells from behind the screen signifying her arrival. Everyone felt very happy on hearing that sound. As I come on the stage slowly dancing, the audience were lost in ecstasy. The Headmaster placed a bottle on My head with a plateful of wick lamps over it and lit the lamps in full view of the audience, lest they may think that the bottle with the plate containing the wick lamps over it was glued to My head earlier, behind the stage. The accompanying musical instruments started playing. I was dancing vigorously. My movements were so fast that the audience completely lost themselves in joy. The moment of climax of the programme had arrived. I danced and finally bent on the stage and lifted the needle planted in the soil, with My eye-lids. The audience clapped their hands loudly and gave Me a standing ovation.

After the end of the programme, the District Collector who was the chief guest for the day's programme wanted to present a medal to Me. He actually wanted to hang it round My neck. He was a Britisher, by name Hasley. But, I was then in the role of Rishyendramani, the female dancer. Hence, I told the organisers of the programme that I cannot allow a male officer touch Me. Is it not a fact that I had to act as Rishyendramani only until the function was over! I told the Collector "You should not touch Me. Please hand over that Medal to Me." The Collector and Myself argued over the matter for a few minutes. He requested Me "you may consider me as your own brother and allow me to decorate the medal round your neck." But, I was firm in My stand. I replied "consider Me as your sister and handover the medal to me." The Headmaster then started prompting from behind the screen "He is a District Collector. Don't go against his wish. Accept his request." Several others also tried to persuade Me in this regard. But, I did not budge even an inch, since My behaviour had to be in conformity with the role I was playing then. Finally, the Collector handed over the medal to me and left the stage. When I retired to the dressing room, there accumulated several envelops addressed to Rishyendramani, some of which contained even money. Some others wrote some nonsensical letters and put them in the envelopes.

The prize distribution ceremony was held the next day, which was presided over by Smt. Rama Subbamma, the then District Board President. She distributed the prizes to all the participants. Thereafter she spoke for sometime. In her speech, she said "Smt. Rishyaendramani had done a great help to our boys and girls. Because of her dance programme today, we have been able to raise enough funds for constructing our school building shortly. Hence, I request her to kindly come on the dais and receive our felicitations." She bought a beautiful silk sari for giving as presentation to her. She called out "Smt.Rishyendramani!" People were anxiously waiting to see from which side Rishyendramani would come. In the meanwhile I ran towards the stage, wearing a knicker and shirt. The Police people tried to push Me away, saying "Rishyendramani is coming; keep yourself aside and give her way." On the other hand, the Headmaster was calling Me to come on the dais. With great difficulty, I could manage to reach the dais. The Headmaster made an anouncement "This is the boy who acted as Rishyendramani yesterday." Rama Subbamma could not contain her joy and lifted Me up and kissed Me. She said "My dear young boy! What a great honour you have brought to this school! I am extremely happy to know that there are people in this country of Bharath who have such a great talent at such a young age. I am really proud of you." From that day onwards, she developed great love for Swami. Wherever she went, she used to describe the greatness of Swami to one and all. The people who attended the dance programme the previous night thought that it was only the famous dancer Rishyendramani that gave the programme. But, the next day they came to know that Rishyendramani did not come at all and this was the boy who gave the performance dressed as Rishyendramani. They were very much surprised and appreciative that this young lad could give such an outstanding performance, as if it was Rishyendramani herself that was dancing. On account of this performance, the school in Uravakonda earned a great name. Wherever one can see, the people were discussing about this incident only.

10
The Sorceror

THE glory of 'Sathyam' was increasing day-by-day in Uravakonda also. Everyday, several people used to come to see Me. Unable to cope with this stream of visitors, Seshama Raju wrote a letter to father that it is no longer possible to keep Me with him. He wrote "It is not possible for us to hold him. You may come immediately and take him away." In those days, it was very difficult for letters to reach from one place to the other. On a particular Monday, Pedda Venkama Raju went to Bukkapatnam to purchase some provisions in the weekly fair. He received Seshama Raju's letter there and straight from the fair, he came to Uravakonda by a bus. Poor man! His pockets were empty, by then. He took some money from Seshamaraju towards bus fare for both of us and started from

Uravakonda. The Bus Service was upto Bukkapatnam only. From there, we had to reach Puttaparthi by walk. Pedda Venkama Raju held My hand and brought Me to Puttaparthi by walk, with great difficulty.

By the time we reached home, Kondama Raju, the grandfather of this body was eagerly awaiting our arrival. He had great faith in gods and goddesses. He told Venkama Raju "Venkappa! Don't take this boy to task. His strange behaviour appears to have a link with Divinity. I will keep this boy with me for sometime." So saying, he kept Me along with him and looked after Me very carefully. Only Venkamma (the elder Sister of this body) out of all the family members was allowed to visit Me daily in the morning and evening. She used to enquire "Sathya! Do you get any dreams? Do you see anyone in your dreams?". But, I used to divert the conversation to some other topic. I was not revealing anything to anybody.

Some people commented "Sathyam is possessed by a ghost. That is why his madness has increased very much. It is not possible for anyone to cure his disease." Yet another person suggested "There is a sorceror in Kadiri, who can cure such diseases. You please take Sathya to him." Then Myself and Venkamma were seated in a bullock cart and taken to Kadiri. Venkamma was not used to leave Me alone, ever for a minute. That sorceror was a big drunkard. He told our people "A ghost has taken over this boy. I will drive it away." So saying, he beat Me severely with a stick, causing injuries to My whole body. I did not give vent to My suffering. I bore it silently. Thereafter, he brought some *Kalikam* (an eye salve that causes severe pain) and put it in My eye. Immediately My eyes became red and greatly swollen. He thought I would submit to him, unable to bear the severe burning and pain in the eyes. But, it did not happen so. That day, in the evening, I told Venkamma to mix some cow-dung in water and pour the mixture in My eyes. She did accordingly. The next day My eyes became normal and white. The sorcerer was frustrated that his efforts were failing. He wanted to make a last ditch effort to drive away the ghost from Me. He got my hair shaved off completely and made two deep cuts on the scalp, with a barber's knife. The blood started oozing out from the cuts, profusely. Then he arranged to pour pots and pots of water on the blood - soaked cuts on the scalp, from a height of about ten feet. Thereafter, he cut some lemons and started massaging those pieces on My head. I did not yield to this torture. Venkamma, who was observing all this process could not, however, contain her emotions. She arranged a bullock cart on that very night and brought Me over to Puttaparthi. Subsequently, Seshama Raju took Me again to Uravakonda and admitted Me in the school, as usual.

11

Ramesh And Suresh

WHEN this body was a student in Uravakonda, three of us, namely Myself, Ramesh and Suresh used to sit on one desk in the class room. Ramesh was the son of a Sirasthadar (a revenue official of the State Government). Suresh was the son of a Revenue Inspector (a State Government official). I used to sit in the middle, with Ramesh and Suresh on either side of Me. Both of them were from well-to-do families to some extent! But, they were very dull in studies, scoring poor marks in all subjects. I used to help them in the class. Whenever the teachers ask them questions, I used to write the answers quickly on a piece of paper and hold it in front of them. They used to read that answer with one eye and repeat it to the teachers and win their appreciation. Thus, I used to help those two boys in many ways. Finally, they came to the conclusion that there is none else except Raju, who can come to their rescue. A lot of transformation took place in their hearts on account of My *Darshan*, *Sparsan* and *Sambhashan* (sight, touch and speech). Their mental relationship with Me has been growing day-by-day. They used to bring some eatables like 'Pakodas' for Me from their houses now and then. But, I used to refuse them saying "I am a person who only gives, but never takes. If there is no give and take relationship between us, then only the friendship between us lasts for ever. If I take anything from you, I will be indebted to you. Hence, I will not take anything from you."

Once, we had to write our ESLC examination. My friends Ramesh and Suresh were very much afraid to face the examination. They approached Me and said "Raju! you alone are our refuge." I told them "What is the use of fearing the examination? Be bold and face the examination." They both requested Me to help them in the examination. I cannot say no when someone seeks My help. I promised to help them. I prepared them one day in advance about the possible questions and the answers for the same. At last, the day of our examination approached. On that day, we had to sit in the examination hall, quite at a distance from one another, as per the seating arrangements. Our roll numbers were so. Hence, there is no possibility at all for them to copy the answers from My answer sheet. Hence, they informed Me that they will not attend the examination. Then, I counselled them, "Having attended the classes till now, it is a mistake to avoid the examination. We have to face them boldly irrespective of the result - whether a pass or a fail. You repose unflinching faith in Me. Face the examination with confidence. The rest, I will look after. I will never let down someone who reposed faith in Me. There are people in this world who tasted failure for lack of faith; but no one has failed in his endeavours, who reposed faith in God. There may be some ups and downs in life sometimes; but ultimately they end up with success in life."

The answer sheets were given to us on the day of the examination. We were not allowed to take anything inside the examination hall. After we entered the examination hall, the Teachers thoroughly checked our pockets for any possible slips and our hands for any writings. It is a common practice for the Teachers in those days to conduct such intense search to find out whether the students wrote some answers on slips of paper or their hands. In the meanwhile, one teacher came there and told the teacher conducting this check: "Kondappa! whom do you think these boys are? They belong to Raju's group. They don't indulge in such malpractices as stealing and copying. They always tread the right path". The teacher Kondappa then replied "I also know about it. The radiance in that boy's face itself reveals the truth." We went into the examination hall. That was the first day of our examinations. Since our roll numbers were quite afar, we three had to sit at a lot of distance from one another. Ramesh and Suresh were therefore very much afraid. Then, I assured them "you don't worry. I will write your answer sheets as well, alongwith mine. They will be in your own handwriting. Just do as I say. I will conduct the rest of the play." I am the Director of the Cosmic Play. The entire universe dances to My tune. Can I not conduct this small playlet? I assured them once again "You do not at all worry about the examination. Since you reposed your faith in Me, I will surely make you successful in the examination." I also revealed to them a plan of action for achieving our purpose. I told them "As you enter the examination hall, you will be given an answer sheet. You will also be given the question paper. You take them and sit in your respective places according to your roll numbers. The rest, I will look after." They used to obey My command in every aspect. They never used to flout My instructions.

As per our plan, Ramesh and Suresh sat in their respective places and pretended to write something. I finished writing My answers in just half-an-hour. I also wrote the answer sheets of Ramesh and Suresh in their respective handwriting in another one hour. Thus, all the three answer sheets were ready in one and a half hours' time. I wrote our names and roll numbers on the concerned answer sheets. In the meanwhile, the bell was rung. The teachers hastned us saying "Time is over; return your answer sheets." All the students got up from their seats and rushed towards the table of the teacher in a group to handover their answer sheets. It was not possible for anyone in that hurried atmosphere to make out who was handing over whose paper. I asked Ramesh and Suresh to go out and placed the answer sheets of all three of us on the teacher's table and silently walked out.

By the time we came out, all the children surrounded us and enquired Ramesh and Suresh as to how did they write the examination, what questions they answered etc. They replied that they wrote something. There was however, one good quality in them; they never spoke lies. They never used to disobey My command. They used to have firm faith in Me. The results of our examinations were anounced after sometime. All three of us secured I class with more than 95% marks. Our Headmaster wrote "Very very very good" on our papers. Since we sat quite afar from each other in the examination hall as per our roll numbers, there is no possibility at all to think that Ramesh and Suresh copied from My answer sheet. Further, our answer sheets were in our respective handwriting, giving no scope for any doubt. Ramesh and Suresh were struck with wonder at My capabilities. They realised that Raju was not an ordinary boy and could do anything. They, therefore, came to Me and expressed their gratitude saying "Raju! It is only because of you, we could get a Ist class."

The citizens of Uravakoda town celebrated that occassion on a grand scale by putting us on their shoulders and taking us in a procession through the streets. Our classmates and their parents as well as several others garlanded us. While we were being taken in procession in the town, Ramesh and Suresh hung their heads in embarassment. I told them "you did not steal anybody's property! Right! Come on! Lift your heads up!" I infused courage and confidence in them. After some time, the teacher asked the same questions that appeared in the examination, in the class room. None of the students could answer them, including Ramesh and Suresh though they secured Ist class in the examinations. I already warned them that they should not reveal to anyone, what had happened in the Examination Hall. I advised them "If anybody makes an enquiry, you just tell him that you wrote whatever that struck to your mind at that time," They did accordingly. Those two boys used to be very close to Me. They had so much love and affection for Me, even at that young age.

12

Visit To Hampi

WHILE I was studying in the Uravakonda School, the chairman of the Municipal Council of Bellary, a neighbouring District headquarters town, had a dream. Somebody told him in the dream "you go to such and such a house in Uravakonda with such and such number and bring that boy 'Sathyam' here". His wife, Laxmidevi, too had a dream at the same time in which some one advised her "Amma! you and your husband go together and bring 'Sathyam' here". Accordingly, both of them came to Uravakonda. I am five feet tall, even now. I was still shorter, then. I was wearing a shirt and knicker then. When I came out from the house one day, the husband and wife saw me. The moment they saw Me, the Chairman and his wife recognised Me as "the boy in the dream". They felt very happy and prostrated before Me in full view of every body in that market place. I was going to the school, with books in hand. The Municipal Chairman approached the brother of this body and requested "Seshama Raju! You think your brother is an ordinary school - going lad. No, No. My heart melted and moved at the sight of the radiance in his face and his purity. There is some inexplicable divine effulgence in this boy. Don't be carried away by a mis-apprehension that this boy is an ordinary boy like any other. We want to take this boy alongwith us and keep him in our house for a few days. You also come alongwith him and stay in our house for a few days. You must bring Sathyam to Bellary, even if it meant applying for leave for a few days." Seshama Raju could not refuse, especially when a person of the status of a Municipal Chairman was requesting him. He went immediately to the Headmaster and requested "Sir! The Chairman Sir is requesting Me to bring Sathyam to Bellary for a few days. I request you to kindly grant me leave for the purpose." The Headmaster had great liking for Me. He told Seshama Raju "You may take Sathyam not only to Bellary, but to any other place. You need not obtain my permission." So saying, he gave his own car and sent us to Bellary.

The Municipal Chairman of Bellary kept us for three days in his house and treated us as honoured guests. Thereafter, he took us to the Virupaksha temple in the world famous Hampi town. What I am now going to relate is not an exaggeration or an egoistic portrayal. All the members of our group entered the Virupaksha Temple. If I say "I don't come into the temple", the brother of this body may pressurise Me to go in or he may get angry for My "impertinence", due to the bodily relationship he had with Me. Hence, I used a little tact and said "My stomach is upset. I don't come into the temple." Our teacher Shri Tammiraju and a group of about fifty to sixty people were accompanying us then. All of them entered into the Virupaksha temple. However, the Municipal Chairman had no other thought except Swami, at that time. I was very young then. Nevertheless, he held My hands and prayed "Please, Raju! you must come! you must come!" I was firm in My opinion. Hence, he could not pressurise Me. Seshama Raju then instructed Me "We will go into the temple, have the *Darshan* of Lord Virupaksha and come back. Till then, you stand guard to our luggage here."

They went inside the temple. At that time, *harathi* (the ritual of burning camphor in front of the deity) to Lord Virupaksha was going on. Surprisingly, they could not find Lord Virupaksha's idol there. Instead, they saw Raju there! Seshama Raju was furious. He thought "Sathyam told me that he will not come into the Temple and stand outside. Thereafter he must have stealthily sneaked into the sanctum-sanctorum and stood behind the idol. What a great sacrilege!" The Municipal Chairman Ramaraju did not, however, think so. He thought "Virupaksha is Raju and Raju is Virupaksha." Seshama Raju came out immediately and searched for Me. I was sitting under the same tree where he kept the luggage. He was a doubting Thomas. He went inside the temple and sent his wife to see whether I was sitting under the tree as usual. She could find Me there. At the same time, Seshama Raju could see Me in the sanctum-sanctorum in place of the idol of Lord Virupaksha. Now, he could confirm to himself that Raju was there in the open as well as in the temple, simultaneously. He felt very happy. But, he could not express his happiness infront of Me, lest it may cause embarassment to him. He tried to explain away the incident by saying to himself "It must have appeared like that due to the anxiety we are undergoing in our minds about Sathyam." The Municipal Chairman who brought us to the Virupaksha Temple had himself experienced this phenomenon of Raju appearing at two places simultaneously. When the group came out of the temple, he held the hands of Seshama Raju and said "Seshama Raju! you are greatly mistaken thinking that Sathyam is your brother. In fact, Sathyam is not your brother. He is not an ordinary individual. There is great 'Divine Power' in him." Then, we were brought from there straight to Bellary. We stayed there for a few days. Ramaraju brought all the officers of the Municipality and

Sri Seshama Raju

Smt. Suseelamma W/o Sri Seshama Raju

The Virupaksha Temple

Lord Virupaksha in the sanctum sanctorum

introduced them to Swami. However, the name 'Swami' was not yet in use in those days. Every one used to call Me "Raju!" Some people even wondered, "How come that this Municipal Chairman is giving so much respect to this young boy?"

Our trip to Bellary and Hampi came to a conclusion and it was time for us to return to Uravakonda. The Municipal Chairman of Bellary wanted to give Me a parting gift. But, I frankly told him that I will not accept any gifts. He offered to get Me four pairs of knickers and shirts. I told him I will not accept even one. There used to be a fashion some fifty years ago for the youth to wear a collar pin to their shirts. You don't find this practice anymore. But, in those days, whoever wears a collar pin was considered to be a great and wealthy person.

He was not sure what kind of gift was to be given to Me, before My departure. His wife advised him that it would be better that a gold collar pin may be presented to Me as a gift. He went to a goldsmith and got one gold collar pin made for Me in an hour's time and put it on the collar of My shirt. He held My hands and prayed "Raju! whenever you see this collar pin, you must remember me." I refused to accept the collar pin. It is My habit not to touch others' articles under any circumstances at any time. Then, Seshama Raju reasoned with Me. "He presented the collar pin out of great love for you. If you refuse, it would amount to insulting him." At last, I accepted the collar pin at the insistence of Seshama Raju and permitted the Municipal Chairman to put it on My collar.

13

The Annunciation

WE returned from Hampi to Uravakonda by a Bus. The next day I had to attend the school. I was going to the school. The collar pin presented by the Municipal Chairman of Bellary dropped on the way as I was walking to the school, holding the books in one hand. It could not be found. But, I was least affected by its loss. Yet, I pretended as though I was anxiously searching for it. Some boys who were following Me enquired, "Raju! What are you searching for?" I told them "You saw me wearing a collar pin, yesterday. That was lost. I am searching for it." They too started searching for the collar pin all over the place. I laughed and remarked "you are going to the school to study. Why are you bothered about the collar pin?" They said "It looked so beautiful when you were wearing it."

One of those boys ran to Seshama Raju's house to inform him about the loss of the collar pin. At that time, Seshama Raju and Rama Raju were discussing among themselves "The actions of Sathyam appear to be very strange. How do we understand his behaviour?" When the boy reported about the loss of the collar pin and My searching for it, they at once rushed to Me. Rama Raju lovingly put his hand round My shoulder and enquired "My dear! what are you searching for?" I replied very innocently "I am searching for something". He understood that there was some inner significance in My reply and further questioned Me "Raju! How is it possible in this world to search for something you do not know?" I then replied, "the collar pin you gave Me dropped somewhere and is not to be found". He said "O.k! Does not matter. I will give you ten such collar pins. Come! Let us go home." Then, I sang the following song, saying "The worldly link had gone, the moment the collar pin is lost."

"It was October twentieth, Sunday,
Baba returned from Hampi and was going to school.
The collar pin dropped and could not be found.
That was the day of change;
The worldly attachment left him in the form of a collar pin.
The pilgrimage to Hampi too served its purpose.
Baba left home saying that Maya
Could not bind him anylonger."

(Telugu Song)

For Me, the worldly attachment was like a pin. And, that has left Me. The Bond got separated. Hence, I left home on the very day. The worldly objects delude us. The day when we come out of this delusion, on the very same day Maya (illusion) leaves us.

In the meanwhile, several people gathered at that place, among whom was an English Teacher by name H.S.Venkata Ramana. I was taken to his house. There they enquired, "Are you searching for God or for the pin?" I replied, "I need not search for God, since he is omnipresent. Neither I need to search for the pin, for, everything is in My hand." Then, Rama Raju questioned Me "Where is God? can we see him?" Earlier, I gave him a ring. It disappeared from his finger and came into My hand. He was stunned. He asked Me "How did it happen?" I replied "I can do anything. Everthing is in My hand." Watching all this, Seshama Raju was astonished and confused. He gave up the feeling that he was the elder brother of this body. Shedding tears of joy, he asked My dear! you are all-knowing. Everything is in your hand. Then, what are you searching for?" I also did not address him as 'brother'! I told him I was no longer bound by worldly relationship. I held the hand of Rama Raju and asked "What is this?" He replied, "It is My hand." Then, I took out the fountain pen from his pocket and asked him "whose pen is this?" He said "It is Mine." "You say that it is my hand, my pen, my body, my mind, my senses etc. The word 'my' indicates that you are different from all this. Then who are you?" I asked him. Then, everyone started thinking, "Yes. What Raju says is correct. We say this is mine and that is mine, but we do not know who we are". Everyone was silent. They agreed that they did not know their true identity. I told them that I had come down only to make people realise their true identity.

It is the eye that sees and the mind that think; (showing the handkerchief), the eye can see this kerchief. But, to identify it as a kerchief, there must be a basis. Is it not? You say this is a kerchief. How did you come to know about it? you say, mind is the basis for all this. What is mind? To whom does it belong? You do not know. You think you know that which is not known to you, in reality. That unknown thing is, infact, your true self. Make efforts to realise it. From that day onwards, many seekers of truth started visiting Me. They used to discuss among themselves; "what Raju says is true. But, how do we realise our true self?" People quote from scriptures and talk high philosophy, but do not know their real meaning. They say "This is my ring; my body; my handkerchief etc. But, they do not realise who that "I" and "My" are. One has to make efforts to realise that truth". I started explaining the concept further: "There are two important aspects one has to consider - one is *drisyam* (that which is seen) and the other is *drashta* (seer). It is said "*yad drisyam thannasyam*" (all that is seen is bound to perish). So, whatever you see is only an illusion. You are the *drashta*, that is your true identity."

The English Teacher H.S. Ramana was a noble soul. His house was on the way to My School. He used to sit in the front veranda of his house and anxiously wait for Me. As soon as he saw Me, he used to call 'Raju', take Me into his house and offer coffee or snacks to Me. But, I was not interested in these worldly objects. Earlier, I used to address him as "Sir!" But, from that day onwards I started addressing him as "Ramana". I told him "You are not My Teacher. Neither I am your student. The teacher-student relationship is worldly. All that the eyes can see and the ears can hear are only worldly. These are perishable. One has to go beyond and search for the transcendental reality." From then onwards, wherever I went and whomever I met, I used to teach these higher principles.

Then, one day Ramana called Seshama Raju and told him, "Seshama Raju! Do not trouble yourself much in trying to understand the behaviour of Sathyam. This boy is delving deeper and deeper into the mysteries of life. It is not possible for anyone to fathom his true nature. Let us wait for sometime and see." So saying, he took Me into his house and offered sancks, coffee, meals etc., with great love. Poor man! He did not realise that I was never interested in such things. I did not touch any of them. In My view, they are all worldly things which undergo constant change. They are not permanent. "You are treating unreal objects as real and striving to achieve them. This is the biggest mistake you are committing." Thus, I taught them higher philosophical concepts. H.S.Ramana used to address Me as "Raju!" till then. From that day onwards, he started addressing Me as "Guruji". Holding My feet, he pleaded with Me "Guruji! Please come to My house." Those who were witnessing the scene were amazed that this elderly gentleman who was a teacher himself was holding the feet of this young boy, his student. Then, Ramana declared in front of all these people. "Not only Me, a day will come when the entire world will fall at his feet."

I told the people gathered there that it was time for Me to leave the house and the school, to embark on My mission to alleviate the suffering of My devotees. I then threw away the books in My hand on the ground and declared thus:

"Know that I am Sai in reality;
Cast off your worldly relationships;
Give up your efforts to restrain Me;
The worldly attachments can no longer bind Me;
None, however great he may be, can hold Me."

(Telugu poem)

Seshama Raju also used to write poetry. He was not in the house when this incident had happened. He came to know about it later through his wife and commented "Somebody made this boy recite this poem; otherwise, how can he compose such a beautiful poem?"

There used to be an Astrologer by name Rama Narayana Sastri, in the neighbouring house. Seshama Raju related all My talk on philosophical truths, to him. He shed tears of joy, on hearing My words. The tears actually fell on My feet. From that day onwards, everybody in Uravakonda started addressing Me as "Sathya Sai Baba." This name, however, was not a new name. Infact, it was an old one. The name given to this body was "Sathya". The visions shown by Me to the people were that of Sai Baba. Hence, they combined these two names and started calling Me "Sathya Sai Baba." I then revealed to the people gathered around Me "I have come to spread the Truth." They were dumb founded on hearing My revelation. I emphasized the point once again saying, "This is not a name which I gave to Myself. Infact, it is you who gave this name to Me! I have no name at all!" So saying, I got up and started walking away. In the meanwhile, all those assembled there including Ramana and Sastri tried to prevent Me from going. I then advised them "Do not try to stop Me. What I expect from you is not outward change. I expect that you undergo mental transformation.

I have come to make you realise your innate truthful nature. I am not this body. Hence, none can restrian Me. Try to follow what I say. Then you will understand your own true nature."

There used to be a big rock in the compound of Anjaneyulu's house. Anjaneyulu was working as an Excise Inspector in Uravakonda. He was a great devotee. I went and sat on that rock. Anjaneyulu used to experience some inexplicable joy and spiritual Aura, in the presence of Swami. His house was in the same street as the school in which I was studying then. He and his wife used to wait at the entrance to their house with some coffee and snacks, waiting anxiously for My arrival on the way to the school. If by any chance their children were there at that time, they used to send them inside the house, lest the couple may have to face some embarassment before their children. As soon as I arrived at their door, they used to prostrate before Me, holding My feet. I used to argue a lot with them saying "Sir! you are older in age. You should not do such things." But, they used to reply "Raju! It is true that we are older in age, so far as the body is concerned. But, we are very insignificant in knowledge and wisdom. You are Lord Krishna, verily." They were afraid that others may make fun of them if they extoll Me like this, in public. Hence, they used to express themselves in private.

I went and sat on the boulder in the garden in the

Sri Anjaneyulu

Sri Ramanarayana Sastri

"Know that I am Sai in reality"

compound of Anjaneyulu's house. He felt very happy saying, "Aha! Raju has come!". He went into his house and told his wife to prepare a variety of dishes. But, I did not touch any of them. I exhorted the people gathered there to sing the bhajan "Manasa Bhajare Guru charanam Dusthara Bhavasagara Tharanam" (Oh! Mind! May you serve the lotus feet of Guru, which will take you across the formindable ocean of samsara.)

All those people gathered there were very much surprised, "How come! what a miraculous change had taken place in this young boy!" Seshama Raju then approached Me and requested Me "Sathya! come let us go home." I replied "I will not come." It was not My nature to disobey the commands of elders. Seshama Raju was therefore surprised that I was for the first time giving a reply to him. He wondered "How did this Sathyam pickup such courage!" While I was looking at him gently smiling with a calm and serene face, he saw great effulgence round My face. While returning from the school, Seshama Raju tried his best to take Me home. But, I told him frankly that I would not come. Anjaneyulu then tried to convince Seshama Raju saying "My dear Sir! you don't trouble him. Let him stay here itself. After sometime when he becomes normal, I will myself bring him home."

In the meanwhile, different types of people gathered there and started questioning Me "Who are you? Are you a devil or a ghost?" I firmly replied in unequivocal terms "I am neither a devil nor a ghost. Know that I am Sai, in reality." They then enquired "How are we to believe that you are Sai Baba?" In those days nobody had ever heard the name 'Sai Baba' in that area. In fact, the name of Sai Baba was not known to anybody in the entire district of Ananthapur. Then someone brought some flowers there. I took those flowers into My hand and threw them on the floor. The flowers arranged themselves as "Sai Baba" in Telugu letters. While I was sitting on that boulder in Anjaneyulu's house, one photographer came there and took a photograph of Me. When it was developed and printed, a small stone in front of Me appeared as Shirdi Sai Baba, in the photo. Copies of that photo were distributed to all the people gathered on that occassion. The boulder on which I sat on that day is still there in Uravakonda. The President of the Andhra Pradesh State, Sathya Sai Seva Organisations, Anjanayya built a beautiful Mandir and a hall in that place. Nobody knew about Sai Baba in those days. When I returned to Puttaparthi from Uravakonda after My annunciation, the villagers heard the name 'Sai Baba', for the first time. They then thought that I had taken upon a Muslim name. But, Sai Baba transcends religion and caste. "Wherever you see, there you will find Him."

"The Vaishnavaites say Vishnu is great;
The Saivaites say Siva is great;

The Ganapathyas say Ganapathi is great;
The Educated say Sarada is great;
The Muslims say Allah is great;
The Saaktheyas say Sakthi is great;
My devotees say Sathya Sai is great;
Yet some others say all forms are one;
However, you must proclaim the truth that all religions are one;
And Brahman is one and only one.
What more can I explain?
Oh! Men of noble qualities assembled here!

(Telugu poem)

Divinity has no particular name or form. Whatever form you contemplate upon, it assumes that form. Did Lord Rama or Lord Krishna incarnate with any particular name? It is only after they incarnated, people gave them names. It is said *Karshatheethi Krishnah*, which means that the one who attracts all people is Krishna. Krishna was really the Embodiment of Bliss.

Who can give a name to the *Atma Thathawa*, which is the embodiment of eternal bliss, wisdom absolute, beyond the pair of opposites, expansive and pervasive like the sky, the goal indicated by the *Mahavakya Thathwamasi*, one without a second, eternal, pure, unchanging and witness to all functions of the intellect.

"The *Atma Thathwa* is immanent in every individual, nay every living being. In fact, I have come into this world only to make people realise this truth" - I explained thus to the people gathered around Me. Seshama Raju then questioned Me "Who are you?" I replied "You are calling Me 'Sathya'. Hence, I am Sathya. If you call Me, 'brother', I am 'brother'. Whoever calls Me by whatever name, I assume that form. To tell you the truth, I have no worldly relationship with anyone. I answer, by whichever name you call Me, All these names are ascribed to Me; they are not the names with which I have taken birth in this world. I have come into this world only to make you realise this truth."

Seshama Raju was utterly confused and dumbfounded at My reply. He did not know what to do in the circumstances. He thought he should send a telegram to the parents asking them to come immediately. But, it took a long time in those days for a telegram to reach Puttaparthi from Uravakonda. Hence, He sent a message through one of his students asking Peda Venkama Raju and Easwaramma to come to Uravakonda immediately. They both came, post-haste. Seshama Raju brought them to the place where I was sitting. Easwaramma cried inconsolably and pleaded with Me "Son! come! let us go to your brother's house." I replied, "I will not come anywhere. If you so desire, I will accompany you to Puttaparthi. I will provide joy to all the villagers of

Puttaparthi and thereafter go to any place of My liking.

In the meanwhile, there was a lot of commotion and enquiry "Where is Raju? Where is Raju?" since I did not attend school that day. None of the boys attended the prayer meeting. All of them rushed to Anjaneyulu's house.

But, I did not look at anybody. I just sat on the boulder looking somewhere. Observing Me, the children started thinking in different ways like "There is a lot of change in Raju. He appears to be mentally deranged. Perhaps, something might have happened in the house after he returned from Hampi." I then advised the children that one of the boys may sing the prayer song in My absence and the school started thereafter.

Twentieth October was the day on which the entire town of Uravakonda underwent a total change. In tune with this, great change had also taken place in the student community. Their love and affection towards Me increased beyond description. A small incident to illustrate the point. I used to sing the prayer song everyday morning in the school assembly. Our Head Master used to appreciate Me very much saying "Raju! Though you are very young, the prayer song you sing stirs our souls." I used to sing the following prayer song daily in the school assembly:

"Moment to moment, thy clarion call resounds-
Hearing thy magnanimous words,
The Hindus, Buddhists, Jains, Parsees, Muslims and Christians,
Come to thy throne, from East and West,
Making the garland of love.
Hail to Thee who unites all humanity!
Hail to Thee who controls the destiny of Bharath!
Hail to Thee! Hail to Thee!

Thus, I taught the unity of all religions in the world even in those days. The prayer song used to be sung in the school everyday morning by one and all including the teachers happily in one voice. After I left the school on that day, one Muslim boy by name Abdul Gafoor was asked to go up the stage and sing the prayer song. He had a melodious voice and could sing well. He went up the stage, but could not sing since he became highly emotional thinking of My separation from him. He wept uncontrollably. The students and teachers also wept, unable to bear My separation. After sometime, the Head Master Lakshmipathi could regain his poise and announced before the assembly, "No more prayer for today. Come, let us depart silently. Our weeping itself, unable to bear the separation of Raju from us, is prayer for today." The prayer ended thus in great agony for everyone and a holiday was declared for the school.

Instead of going home, all the teachers and students gathered round the house where I was staying. Several students came to Me and started reminding Me of their acquaintance with Me saying, "Raju! Do you remember me? I used to sit behind your desk." But I did not look at their faces, even. They were very much disappointed and wept inconsolably and left for their homes. That was really a pathetic scene. But, I acted like that purposely, with a view to bring about a change in them. Since then, the students are continuously after Swami. The students of those days were so pure in their heart and innocent. They never used to indulge in any sort of criticism, impertinent questions or evil thoughts. In contrast, the students of the present times are becoming more and more intelligent, with noble qualities decreasing day by day. In those days, they were less in intelligence and more in good qualities. Finally when I started to return to Puttaparthi, all the boys insisted on accompanying Me. In those days, there were no Buses plying to Bukkapatnam, at least. They were plying upto Penukoda only. From there one has to reach Puttaparthi, by a bullok cart. That was the state of transport facilities in those days. The children were not prepared to listen to anyone. They insisted "We will also go with Raju". How could this small village of Puttaparthi accommodate so many people? I, therefore, requested the Head Master to convince those boys not to come to

Puttaparthi. I boarded the Bus. The Headmaster also shed tears at the time of My departure. Everyone present there felt very sorry that I was leaving. But, I did not give importance to their feelings. I am not one to be carried away by such emotions. I should not.

Thus, while I was coming away from Uravakonda, two boys who used to sit on the same desk alongwith Me in the school, ran after Me calling "Raju! Raju!" From then on, My very form had changed. My words had changed. I was questioning them "What is the relationship between us? From where did you come? Who are you? Who am I?" When Ramesh and Suresh observed My strange behaviour, they were mentally upset. With great mental agony, they yearned for Me calling "Raju! Raju! Raju!" The Bus started. Unable to bear the separation, Ramesh, the son of Sirasthadar ran towards a well nearby and committed suicide by jumping into it. He thought to himself "I don't want to live without Raju". The second boy became mad, always babbling "Raju! Raju! Raju!" Day in and day out, he was talking to himself "Raju! why did you leave us? Why did you leave us?" He did not take food and water and always chanted My name for days on end. This type of madness is nothing but spiritual yearning. This boy Suresh was then taken to Bangalore and admitted in a Mental Hospital. His father approached Me and prayed "Swami! He was sitting by your side on the same desk in your classroom in Uravakonda High School. He is my only son. Please come once and see him." I told him "That boy Suresh was different. This Suresh is a different one. No useful purpose will be served by My coming." But, the boy's father insisted. Hence, I had to go to Bangalore and see the boy in the Mental Hospital. He was constantly chanting "Raju! Raju!" He was not looking at anybody. I called him by his name and told him "Suresh! I am Raju. I have come to see you."

Immediately, he lifted his head and saw Me. Thereafter, he closed his eyes and died peacefully. Both Ramesh and Suresh used to tell Me always "Raju! we wish to be with you always. We cannot bear the separation from you, even for a moment. After both these boys died in such tragic circumstances, the classroom in which all three of us used to sit on a desk, was locked permanently. The desk on which we three used to sit is there even now. It was christened as "Sri Sathya Sai Baba desk." All the students in the school used to love Me as their very life-breath. I also used to reciprocate My love, so intensely. I used to share the *Vadas*, *Pakodas* etc., prepared in our house with them. Infact, Ramesh and Suresh gave up their lives for the sake of Swami's love. Some one asked Me later "Swami! you wrote the examination paper on their behalf and put their names on their answer sheets. How come?" I replied, "Ramesh is also My name. Similarly, the name Suresh also belongs to Me. All names and forms are Mine." When I answered thus, they could not say anything further. Thus, if I go on narrating 'My story', there will be no end to it.

Dear Students! when I was a student in those days, I used to help everyone, provide happiness and joy to everyone and be jovial with every one. Since you are students of Sri Sathya Sai Institute of Higher Learning, you emulate My example and help everybody and share your joy with everybody.

14
Jack And Jill

WHEN I was residing in the old Mandir, there used to be one British couple by name Mr. and Mrs. Krupp. One day, they brought two puppies named Lilly and Billy and requested Me "Swami! These puppies are born in our house. We wish to keep them in Swami's divine presence. Eventhough we are not here physically, we feel satisfied that we are living in Swami's divine presence if Swami can kindly keep these puppies with Him." I agreed to their request and kept those puppies with Me. In course of time, they gave birth to two puppies. I named them Jack and Jill. They were none other than Ramesh and Suresh, who were My classmates earlier. Unable to bear My separation, they died and were reborn as these puppies to live in My presence. I was living in the old Mandir, then. They had so much love for Swami that they used to be with Me always. Even while I was sleeping, they used to be with Me, one by the side of My head and the other at My feet. They never used to sleep during night. They used to keep themselves awake the whole night, barking at the sight of any person. Thus, they used to be with Me always.

After sometime, the Maharani of Mysore came to Puttaparthi to have My *darshan.* She was an orthodox woman. She never used to touch anyone. Not only that. She was not even touching the articles touched by others. If she required cow's milk, the cow had to be first bathed and then only milked. She was so much orthodox. She never used to take food even, if some dogs barked. Hence, her secretary used to visit the *Asram* before her and inform the people there, "if there are any dogs here, kindly keep them in a room and put a lock to it." There used to be no motorable road to Puttaparthi, in those days. Hence, she had to get down from the car at Karnata Nagepalle and then walk the distance upto the old Mandir in Puttaparthi. She did not like to walk in other's footsteps. Hence, she brought four wooden planks in a van behind her car. First, they used to put two planks on the path and she used to step on them. Then, the next two planks are placed and she would place her feet on them. Thus, the process was repeated and finally she arrived at the Mandir and had Swami's *darshan.* She was a great devotee. In those days, there used to be no hotels anywhere near Karnata Nagepalle. Hence, the driver had to come to the Mandir for dinner in the night. The Maharani told the driver "I wish to sleep one night in the Mandir premises. Hence, I will not return today."

The driver, however, had to return to the place where he kept the car, after dinner. That was already dark. There were no electric lights in the street. Puttaparthi was a remote primitive village, sixty years ago. In the same primitive village, one Airport, University and Railway Station are established today. But, there were not even good roads then. I called Jack and instructed "go with the driver to help him in finding the way." The driver was surprised "How come! Can this dog show me the way?" Then, I told the driver, "the god in this dog will show you the way." While the dog Jack was walking ahead, the driver followed it. He slept in the car for that night. There was heavy rain then. Hence, the dog slept under the car near the tyre. The driver woke up early in the morning. That was winter season. Hence, the driver wanted to start the car and run it for a short distance to ensure that the engine is in perfect condition before the Maharani comes out to resume her return journey. He started the car and the tyre moved over the back of the dog, Jack. Her spinal chord was broken. See! How faithful was that dog! The students, teachers and devotees - everyone should note this point carefully. Unable to bear with the excruciating pain on account of its broken spine, Jack started moving towards the Mandir. It had to cross the river Chitravathi dragging its body somehow through the sand. It was profusely bleeding.

There used to be a washerman by name Subbanna near the entrance to the old Mandir. He came running into the Mandir and informed Me "Swami! Our Jack's back is broken. It is coming here groaning with great pain." I came out and went near the dog calling "Jack! Jack!" It was crying with uncontrollable pain and fell at My feet, the moment it saw Me. See! How faithful it was! It wanted to breathe its last, falling at My feet. Therefore, it dragged itself to My feet from such a long distance, inspite of the great pain it was undergoing. I arranged for some milk from the Mandir and poured the milk into the mouth of Jack. After drinking the milk, it lifted its two front legs and put them on My hand and breathed its last, looking at Me faithfully. I arranged for its burial in the backyard of the old Mandir. However, I told the people to bury it to a side, so that enough space is available for another Samadhi. Unable to bear with the separation of Jack, the other dog Jill gave up eating food and died after a few days. Jill was buried next to the Samadhi of Jack. Thereafter, I got one Tulasi Brindavan built in that place. It used to be there till very recently. When the renovation of the old Mandir was taken up for the purpose of rebuilding a Kalyana Mandapam in that place, the Tulasi Brindavan has been removed. I was in Bangalore then. Thus, Ramesh and Suresh always wanted to be near Swami and even took birth as dogs for the purpose. They finally merged in Swami. Their story reminds about the truth that those who are faithful to God will never be lacking in anything.

What a great faith! what a great love those dogs had towards Swami! Even if a fraction of their faith and love is there in a human being, his life would have been sanctified. Unfortunately, today man lacks such faith. People have unending desires; but who is living upto the ideals of Swami? How is it possible for your desires to be fulfilled, if you give up the ideals? What you have to learn is, whatever difficulties you may undergo, never keep yourself away from God's Love. If you hold on to God's love steadfast, even mountainous difficulties will melt away like ice.

15

Subbamma's Devotion

THERE used to be a great devotee by name Karanam Subbamma, in Puttaparthi. She was rich and noble in qualities. She had no children. Whatever she had, she used to give away in charity to one and all with a feeling, "I am only sharing my God-given wealth with my fellow human beings." She used to spend her time with such sacred thoughts and equanimity of mind. She always used to call Me "Sathya! Sathya!" and come near Me. But, I was not immediately going to her house, the moment she called Me. Then, she used to plead with Me in a humble tone, "My dear! why should you not come to our house?" I used to reply "I am not a beggar to come to your house, without an invitation. If you call Me, I will come, otherwise, I won't. One day, Subbamma called Me and said "Raju! I have prepared dosas today. You kindly come to our house and partake some". In those days, eatables like dosas and iddlies were not available in everybody's house. Only some rich people used to prepare them in their houses. I told Subbamma "I can't leave all these children and come alone to partake of the dosas in your house." Poor lady! Then she prepared dosas for all the children.

One day all of us went to Subbamma's house. She was a very pious housewife and a broadmined lady. She felt a little embarassed on seeing all the children, since she was not prepared for our visit. She, therefore, requested Me, "Raju! you have brought the children to my house. Very good. But, I did not prepare any item and kept it ready for the children. You please bring all these children tomorrow. I will prepare some eatables and keep them ready." The next day she prepared the dish of My liking, namely a soup made out of "Pithiki Bedalu" (a particular variety of pulse - *phaseolus radiatus*). All the children including Myself sat for lunch. I warned the children in advance. "Subbamma belongs to the Brahmin community. It is difficult for them to caste away the differences on account of caste and religion. Hence, keep some distance from her as far as possible." She brought some rice mixed with the soup, in a vessel. She dropped morsel after morsel of this food, in the hands of each of these boys. All of them ate to their hearts' content. I was very happy on seeing the boys eating well. She realised the truth then that Raju would feel satisfied only when the children are fed well. That is why, she fed the children first. Finally, a very small quantity of the food was left in the vessel. She felt very unhappy that she could not provide enough quantity for Me. Whatever little quantity of food was left over, she put it in My mouth. On observing this, the children started whispering into one another's ears "why did she feed only Raju in this manner by putting it into his mouth whereas for all of us, she dropped it into our hands?" I could gauze the situation. I told Subbamma "Look! The children seem to be a bit agitated by your actions." Subbamma then explained the whole matter in a beautiful way to the children thus: "My dear children! It is not that I don't love you as much as I love Raju. In fact, Raju will feel happy and contented only when you eat first. Such was his love towards you. That is why I fed you first. Finally, only a little quantity of food is left over. It cannot be made into morsels and dropped into Raju's hands, one by one. That is why I put it into his mouth. Raju's nature is to satisfy others' hunger first. He feels satisfied when they eat fully. You cannot find even a trace of selfishness in Raju. You must also become like Raju. You must leave selfish interests, cultivate love and consider others' happiness as your happiness. Then only you will prosper. Your future will be bright and your life will be an ideal to others." So saying, she diffused the situation tactfully, sending Me on an errand to get her some curry leaves. She told Me "Raju! I will prepare "chitrannam" (a sort of rice preparation) for myself for this evening. Please go and get some curry leaves from that tree." I was older in age to all the children gathered there, but I was shorter than all of them. However, I had the knack of climbing the trees easily. I climbed the tree and collected some curry leaves, as desired by Subbamma. But, do you know the actual reason why she sent Me to bring some curry leaves?

She took the opportunity to explain about My greatness and noble qualities to the children. She told them "My dear children! How fortunate you are to have Raju as your close friend! Raju is not an ordinary boy. He is king of kings. He will prove himself to be so in course of time. You obey his command implicitly. Never disobey his command under any circumstances. Never be angry with him. If you are angry with him, the *devathas* (Gods) will be angry with you. You make him happy and derive happiness thereby. If Raju is dissatisfied for any reason, he will not disclose his feelings to anybody. But, you will surely reap its consequences. Hence, always make Raju happy and keep him satisfied." Subbamma's husband had a second wife by name Kamalamma. She approached Subbamma and enquired "What dear elder sister! How do these small children understand the philosophy you are teaching?"

Subbamma replied to her query saying "This is not philosophy, My dear younger sister! I am teaching to these young children, certain 'do's' and 'don'ts' to be observed by them in their day-to-day life. Since I have no children, I consider these children only as my children. These boys move constantly with Raju. And, Raju is my very life-breath."

One day, she prepared *vadas* in her house. But, they were not sufficient in quantity to be served to all the children. Hence, she wanted to share some with Me, exclusively. She went near the window for the purpose. Her very next house belonged to the parents of this body. She called Me through the window "Raju! Raju! please come here once." I went near the window. She tried to pass on through the window, a small packet containing some *vadas*. Then, I told her "Subbamma! It is not fair on your part to give *vadas* to Me only, leaving away the children. You must broaden your heart." Subbamma replied "Please excuse Me for today, Raju! From tomorrow, I will distribute to all the children equally." I then took the *vadas* from her and distributed to all the children in small pieces, in the evening.

You can not understand even one thousandth part of My loving nature, equal-mindedness and divinity. My love is expansive. However much you may try to describe it, it still becomes inadequate. Most people do not ever make any effort to understand My love. *Lokah*

Samasthah Sukhino Bhavanthu (Let the whole world be happy) is My motto. "All people must be happy; no one should undergo difficulties," is My wish.

The dropping down of the collar pin, leaving the school for ever and the parents requesting Me to come back to Puttaparthi - these are all the reasons which prompted Me to come away from Uravakonda permanently. Since then, My glory has been increasing day by day. People from the neighbouring villages started coming to Puttaparthi in large numbers in bullock carts to seek remedies for various types of ailments - mental and physical. They used to bring persons with various types of mental diseases and those allegedly possessed by devils and ghosts. They used to think with great faith in Me. "It seems the devils and ghosts would leave if this boy orders them so." True to their faith, the moment such 'patients' are brought to My presence, they are relieved of the devils and ghosts. On witnessing this miracle, several people believed My words to be true. Venkamma, the elder Sister of this body developed great faith in Sai Baba. She requested Me "Sathya! I want a photo of Sai Baba. Please give me one." Then, I created one photo and gave it to her. She kept the photo with her till her last breath.

The miraculous power of Sai has been growing day by day and hundreds of devotees from far and wide started visiting Puttaparthi everyday. The people in the house could not make arrangements for their stay and food. Pedda Venkama Raju then requested the visiting devotees, “Please come here only once a week, that is, on every Thursday.” The devotees were very much disappointed and agitated. They protested, “How is it possible? How are we to wait till a Thursday? In the meanwhile, our diseases may turn serious.” Our neighbour Subbamma then intervened and suggested “Venkappa! your house cannot accommodate the hundreds of devotees visiting this boy daily. Please, therefore, send him to our house. I will look after the needs of this boy as well as the devotees visiting him. She also requested Me “Swami! I don’t have children. I consider service to the devotees as service to God. I cook food to all the devotees coming here and serve them. Kindly stay in our house only.” From that day onwards, she used to cook food to all the devotees visiting Me and serve them day and night. In fact, Subbamma’s love towards Me is more than what Yasoda had towards Krishna, in the Krishnavathar. Eswaramma and Subbamma were neighbours and they had great love and affection for one another. But, the men in the families were not on talking terms with each other. Easwaramma was not allowed to visit Subbamma and she, in turn, was forbidden from visiting her neighbour. Hence, they both used to communicate with each other through the window.

One day I told Subbamma, “Subbamma! you arrange to get one orange-coloured gown stitched for

Me." She asked Me "Swami! if you wish, you wear a *dhoti*. Why should you have to wear a gown?" I replied "No, No. I am asking you to get one orange-coloured gown, since the time has come for Me to wear ochre robes. She did not want to say 'no' to Swami's instructions. Hence, she got one gown stitched for Me and brought it. The cost of the cloth for gown in those days was two annas. The stitching charge was one quarter of anna (Bottu). Thus, with two annas and a quarter, a gown was ready for Me. As soon as I wore the gown, she called Easwaramma. Easwaramma came and shed tears on seeing Me in those ochre robes. She said "What Swami! Is it for witnessing this form, you called Me here? Enough, enough." I convinced them saying "It is only to remove the *kashaya* (evil feeling and bitterness) from the minds of the people, I wore this *Kaashaaya* (Ochre robes).

Subbamma belonged to the Brahmin caste, whereas this Sai Baba belonged to the Kshatria caste. Hence, the entire Brahmin community in the village of Puttaparthi decided unanimously "This lady kept Sai Baba in her house. We should not, therefore, go to her house nor allow her to visit our house." Subbamma was not bothered about their decision. She told her community people firmly, "I don't need anybody. Nor I need visit anybody's house. You may do whatever you like. I will not leave this boy under any circumstances."

Smt. Karanam Subbamma

Smt. Karanam Kamalamma

The house of Smt. Karanam Subbamma

She did not like to be away from Swami, even for a moment. She used to treat Swami as her own child. With the result, the entire Brahmin community bore grudge against her. But, Subbamma did not budge an inch. She knew that she had to face such difficulties in matters relating to spirituality.

In a very short time, the number of people visiting Me increased by leaps and bounds, with the result that Subbamma's house was also not sufficient to accommodate them. On observing the position, Pedda Venkama Raju suggested to Subbamma "Revered Mother! Why should you have to be inconvenienced on account of our boy? Hereafter, let us keep Sathyam in a separate house." Subbamma then donated a piece of land adjacent to the Venugopala Swami's Temple, where a small room was built exclusively for Me. Subbamma also donated some amount for the purpose. They used to keep Me in that room and lock it from outside. Yet, I used to get away from that room somehow every now and then and go up the nearby hill where I used to sit for long hours. Everyone used to be surprised, "How did this happen? The lock we put to the door is intact. Then, how could this boy come out?" Such miracles were happening almost daily.

One night, some people who did not like Me locked the door of My room from outside and set it on fire. At that time, I was sleeping in that room. Also, some ten children slept in the adjacent verandah. On seeing the flames, they started shouting "Raju! Raju!" The door could not be opened, since it was locked from outside. I opened the doors of a small window from inside the room. The children saw Me laughing. I tried to instill courage in them, saying "you don't worry at all! It is said '*Dharmo Rakshathi Rakshithah!* Since we are protecting *Sathya* (Truth) and *Dharma* (righteousness), they will in turn protect us." The children however, got panicky. They just closed their eyes shouting "Raju! Raju!" In fact, that was the *manthra* they were chanting continuously. In the meanwhile, a number of people arrived there, fearing for My life. Venkamma, Subbamma, Easwaramma and all the family members rushed there, crying. In a few seconds, there was a down pour. But, surprisingly there was no rain at all at any other place except that small hut. The flames subsided on account of the heavy rain. Everyone was happy that Swami was safe. They felt very sad, thinking "Some evil-minded and wicked people might have been indulging in such heinous acts." Subbamma then got the lock broken and took Me to her house.

Subbamma liked Swami verymuch. In fact, Swami was her very life-breath. The entire land in Puttaparthi used to be in her name, those days. She arranged for an enquiry into who were responsible for setting Swami's room on fire. Some five or six people were identified and held in custody. She thundered "you wicked fellows! you should not remain in this village. Leave this village forthwith and go away". Then I pleaded with her holding her hands "Subbamma! They should not suffer on account of Me. Knowingly or unknowingly, they committed a mistake. Please pardon them. Do not send them away from the village." They all approached Me and carried Me on their shoulders, profusely shedding tears of joy and repenting for their misdemeanor. The group consisted of Subbanna, who sells liquor and one Ramanna, besides some other people . They expressed "you did great merit in some previous birth. Otherwise, there is no scope at all for such noble qualities manifesting in you. This village will earn great reputation in due course, on account of you. Subbamma then declared "You consider this boy as an ordinary village urchin. He is not a boy. He is a Thunderbolt, verily."

From that day onwards, Subbamma did not allow Me to go outside. She kept Me in her own house. She was then sixty years old. She was always chanting My name. She could not sleep if I was not found in her vicinity. Oneday, she called the mothers of the ten children who used to be constantly in My company and told them "From today, these children are not only yours; they also belong to Me. All these children will be here with our Raju." Those ten friends were living till very recently. You too know about Bukkapatnam Sathayanarayana. He was My classmate. Several such children used to be in My company. One can not describe how pure and unwavering their love was! Unfortunately today, evil intentions and bad thoughts are inceasing in the children due to the effect of modern age.

Bukkapatnam Sathyanarayana was also a good-natured person. One day, My shirt got torn. He saw the condition of the shirt. In those days, a piece of cloth sufficient for a pair of shirt and knicker used to cost only one and a half annas. He brought the cloth nicely packed in a paper and requested Me "Raju! If you don't think otherwise, I brought this cloth for you with great love. You must get a pair of shirt and knicker stitched out of the cloth." I refused the packet of cloth saying "If you feel that the relationship between you and Me shall last forever, you should not offer this cloth to Me. I will not even touch this packet." In fact, I had never taken even a paisa from any one so far. I don't need anything. Whatever I need, it will come to Me of its own accord. Hence, I have no necessity to stretch My hand before anybody. My hand is always above that of others. It is never below. This has been so, right from My childhood and will continue to be so. I take pleasure in giving, not taking. Some jealous people may accuse Me that I did not give anything to them. But, I do not give credence to such criticism. I never hated or acused or derided anybody. I used to wish happily even those who derided Me.

There was another lady in the village, who was the wife of a prominet person. She did not like Subbamma. She was angry that I was regularly going to the house of Subbamma and not visiting her house. She decided, "This boy must be killed somehow". One day she accosted Me, saying "My dear! Today you must come to our house for breakfast. Don't reveal this to anybody. You should come alone. I will prepare tasty *vadas* for you." She came to the house of Subbamma and requested "Subbamma! Please send Raju to our house today, for breakfast." But, Subbamma did not like that idea. She suspected that, that lady had an evil plan in her mind. She approached Me and said "Raju! she is inviting you to her house, with some evil intention. You please don't go." I was however, determined to visit her house. I told Subbamma, "Come what may, I must fulfill her wish." I went to her house. She prepared *vadas* mixed with poison and brought for My consumption. I knew they were mixed with poison. Yet, I ate them. Within five minutes, My blood was poisoned and the entire body turned into blue colour. Some people who observed this rushed to the house of Subbamma and informed her and Easwaramma about the incident. They came running. I told them, "You don't worry. She did what she wanted to. Now, I will do what I have to do." So saying, I asked them to bring some water in a tumbler. As soon as I took the tumbler into My hands, the entire quantity of water in it turned blue.

Having come to know of the incident, the villagers attacked the house of that lady. Kondama Raju also became furious. He called some *Boyas* (people belonging to the hunting community) and told them to teach a lesson to that lady. Then, I went near Kondama Raju and gently told him "Grandfather! you are an elderly gentleman. You should not prompt them to do such things. It is not proper to indulge in violence against others, especially a lady. If anyone tries to harm her, I will leave this house and stay in her house only, hereafter.

Thus, it is only after I came out unscathed from several such tests, people started believing Me as Sai Baba. In the meanwhile, one person started calling himself a devotee of Sai Baba. Yet some others imitated My hair style and started wearing a gown like Me and called themselves Sai Baba. Is it possible to gain the confidence of people merely by adopting such tactics? Very soon, people realised their efforts as deceit. They came to know the truth.

Gradually, eminent people like the Maharani of Mysore and some other big people started coming to Puttaparthi in cars to see Me. The Chitravathi river was flowing perennially in those days. They used to park their cars on the other side of the river and come to Puttaparthi wading through the knee-deep water. Thus, when devotees from for and wide started coming to Puttaparthi with great devotion to have My *darshan*, *sparshan* and *sambhashan*, none could create any more hurdles in the spread of My mission. The name and fame of Swami spread to far-off lands.

After the death of her husband, Subbamma dedicated her entire life to the service of Swami. Till her last breath, she spent her time in the service of Swami. In fact, there is a lot to be learnt about her devotion and surrender to Swami, by you. She used to provide free food to all the devotees visiting Swami. Oneday, we were travelling in a bullock cart. I asked her "Subbamma! what do you want?" she hesitated a bit and looked this side and that side. Having realised that there was none nearby she told Me "Swami! I don't want anything. However, at the time of my departure from this earthly sojourn, please pour a few drops of water into My mouth, with your divine hands." I promised her that I would certainly fulfill her request.

The entire property of the village of Puttaparthi used to be in her name. She was the head of the entire village. Everyone in the village used to respect her. However, ever since she came into the fold of Swami, she had no other interest in life except Swami. Right from early morning till she went to bed, she was constantly engaged in Swami's work only. On certain occassions, I used to retire into the caves of the nearby hills without informing her. Poor lady! She used to go round the hills in search of Me. She used to pack *upma*, *dosa*, *vada*, *iddly* etc. in a tiffin carrier and come in search of Me. At last, when she could find Me, I used to enquire her teasingly "Subbamma! what did you bring for Me? She used to reply "Swami! I brought the items of your taste". Then, I used to tell her "give Me *dosa*". She would then serve *dosa* in a plate and hand it over to Me. I used to tease her further saying "Subbamma! I don't like this *dosa*. Give Me *iddly*, *upma*, *vada* etc." Poor lady! she used to serve Me all those items. From morning till evening, she used to prepare a number of items and wait for Me. Yet, she was anxious to know what more I needed. Once I told her "Subbamma! you need not feel anxious. I don't need anything. I have put so many questions to you asking for this and that with a view to make your devotion and spirit of surrender known to the world." Subbamma then requested Me, "Swami! please put a little quantity of the item you have tasted, in My mouth." Then I took a small piece of iddly from My plate and put it in her mouth, with a little chutney. Thus, Subbamma experienced great bliss in the divine proximity of Swami, till her last breath.

The washerman in the village, Subbanna had great strength. Another person by name Subbanna, son of

Chandrappa was hefty with seven feet height. Subbamma imposed a condition that one of them should always accompany Me. She told them "Baba sleeps in the Mandir. He will be alone. One of you should always be there day and night, by turns. He will also be going to the river, whenever he pleases. He is a young boy. He cannot walk. Hence, you should carry him on your shoulders and take him wherever he wants." Thus, she used to make several arrangements for My convenience. She had broad-mindedness. Whatever she did, she did it to please Swami.

The Harijans in the village had great liking for Swami. Every now and then, they used to take Swami to their houses. Subbamma also used to come to their houses along with Me. One day, one Harijan by name Gangappa invited Me for lunch in his house. I told Subbamma that I was going to the house of Gangappa for lunch. Subbamma said that she would also come with Me. I told her "I am going to take My lunch in the house of a Harijan. You should not come." Subbamma insisted saying "What Swami! If you are going why not I? I don't have such differences. I will also come." She came alongwith Me. We took our lunch in that house. Gangappa was very much afraid of the consequences saying "How did it happen? Subbamma Madam had come to our house for lunch. I told him "you don't be afraid. You are Harijans (children of Lord Vishnu). Shed your differences of religion and caste and live happily with unity among all people."

Thus, right from My childhood, I strove to remove such differences in the society. If I go on narrating like this, it will become a voluminous history. First and foremost, each one of you cultivate love. The one devoid of love is equal to a dead body. Never keep youself away from love, under any circumstances. If not here today, you have to think of Me somewhere and at sometime. Wherever you are, I have to come to your rescue. What is the use of not realising this truth and repenting later? Instead, realise the truth now itself and conduct yourself accordingly. Cultivate love. Realise the truth, "love is our life" and conduct yourself accordingly.

When I was residing in the old Mandir, we used to go to the Chitravathi river daily. All the children in the village used to accompany Me. One boy used to ask for a pencil and another, a pen. Since they were children, they used to ask for such articles. I used to tell them "make a heap of sand and search for the article of your choice in that heap." They used to get in that sand, whatever they wanted. One day, we were returning from the Chitravathi river to the old Mandir. Suseelamma and her sister Kumaramma (the author of the book 'Anyatha Saranam Naasthi') ran in advance to the Mandir, with a view to make arrangements for giving *harathi* (waving of camphor flame) to Swami. Then, I made a signal to Subbamma to stop those two ladies. I told her, " you go to the Mandir first." Then, she stopped them and said, "you stay here itself. I will go in advance." The two sisters wondered "Subbamma is a widow. How can she give *harathi* to Swami?" When Subbamma reached the entrance door of the old Mandir, she found a big snake there. Subbamma used to look after everything in the Mandir carefully. She addressed the snake as "Sai Nageswara! Sai Nageswara!" with a loud voice. In the meanwhile, all people ran to that place. Subbamma thought to herself, "Swamy says God is immanent in every living being. Hence, this snake should not be beaten or killed." She held the snake courageously with her hand. Immediately it coiled round her hand, instead of biting her. I reached that place by that time. I jocularly enquired "Subbamma! Are you playing with the snake?" She replied "Swami! Is it not for rescuing those ladies that you sent me here in advance?" Thus, Subbamma was a witness to several such miracles. She was a noble, pious and a very fortunate lady. She did great service to Me, right from the beginning. Not only to Me, she used to cook food for all the devotees visiting Me. With the result, all her relatives bore a grudge against her. But, she did not care. She used to declare, "I don't need anybody. It is enough if only Swami is by My side. Whatever He says, I will obey it, implicitly." She used to have such firm faith in Swami.

One day, I enquired her, "Subbamma! would you like to see your late husband?" I used to cut jokes with her like that, now and then. By that time, her husband had already died. She replied, "Swami! I have no such desires, What connection do I have with a person who is no more? He was not destined to witness your glory. Therefore, he died. I have the good fortune. Hence, I am able to serve you." But, I prompted her a little more to agree to My suggestion. I told her "If you wish to see him just once, you may do so. You will be relieved of that obligation as well." I told her to go out into the backyard of her house and watch. There used to be a plant yielding drum-sticks (*Hyperanthera morringa*) there. Subbamma witnessed a scene there, where her husband the late Narayana Rao was sitting under the tree and smoking a cigarette. She was happy to see her late husband in flesh and blood, again. At the same time, she was also very angry that he did not give up his old habits even after death. With utter disgust, she told him "you did not leave your bad habits even after death! Strange! I don't even see your face." So saying, she came back into the house. Subbamma's husband had a second wife by name Kamalamma. She is here in the Prasanthi Nilayalam Mandir, even now. I called her and told her "Kamalamma! you may also go and see your late husband once." But, she refused saying, "Swami! We are here in your divine presence, happily spending our time. We don't wish for anything else." I, however, insisted and said "Just go once, see him and come back." When Kamalamma went in and saw him, he was drinking hot coffee! He was indulging in the same actions as he used to do when he was alive. Thus, Lord Krishna also showed some incidents of the bygone era to his contemporaries.

Subbamma engaged herself in the service of Swami, till her last breath. Though she had no bodily relationship with Me, she used to have intimate relationship with Me, mentally and spiritually. She was constantly contemplating on Me. She requested Swami to stay in her house only. In fact, she offered to vacate her house and give it to Swami. Her relatives argued with her, "You are a Brahmin lady and he is a Kshatriya boy. Why do you allow him into your house?" She stoutly refuted their argument and firmly declared, "I don't need any of you. I will not come to your houses nor you need come to My house. If only Swami is with Me, that is enough for Me." She had only one desire to be fulfilled by Me. She prayed, "Swami! During My last moments of life, I must have the good fortune of witnessing your beautiful face." I promised her that her wish will be fulfilled. Once, the devotees from Madras (Chennai) pressurised Me to visit that place, urgently. Those were the days of second world war. Once in every hour, there used to be air raid precautionary siren blowing and the streets would become empty in no time. I could not return to Puttaparthi early, in those circumstances. In the meanwhile, the condition of Subbamma turned serious. She was taken to her parents' house in Bukkapatnam. She breathed her last there itself. Her body was kept in the front verandah, covered with a cloth. All the members of the family were immersed in sorrow. Her mother and relatives were very sad. The relatives started talking in several ways "Sai Baba gave a word that he would pour a few drops of water in her mouth before she breathed her last. Now, she really breathed her last. But, where is Sai Baba? He did not come even to have a last look at her. No one knows where he has gone!"

In those days, there was no motorable road to Puttaparthi. I had to come to Bukkapatnam by car from Madras and from there to Puttaparthi in a bullock cart. By the time I reached Bukkapatnam, I noticed several people gathered on the road. They appeared to be in a sorrowful mood. I enquired one gentleman, "What happened?" He replied "Swami! yesterday night, Karanam Subbamma left her body. Till her last breath, she was chanting 'Sairam! Sairam!' They are now making arrangements for taking her body to the burial ground". In those days, firewood and such other articles to cremate a dead body were not available in the village as 'ready-made' items. Hence, some firewood was collected from here and there and everything was made ready to take her body to the burial ground. I enquired someone "Where is Subbamma now?" He replied "Swami! Her dead body is kept in the veranda of her mother's house." I had a hearty laugh. I did not forget My promise to Subbamma, nor did she. I asked the bullock cart driver to take it to Subbamma's house. There, all arrangements were being made to take her body to the burial ground. All the people gathered in the veranda were weeping. They told Me "Swami! Subbamma was remembering you and chanting your name only, till her last breath." Then I enquired, "Where has she gone?", as if I did not know anything. They informed Me "Swami! The Doctors came here and examined her. They confirmed that there was no life in her." Since they were Brahmins, they did not allow anybody to come near Subbamma's dead body. Subbamma's mother and sisters wept loudly, the moment they saw Me. They started showering ironical praise on Me saying "Baba! Subbamma had great hopes till her last moment that you will come and pour a few drops of water in her mouth. She anxiously waited for your *darshan*. Finally, she breathed her last, greatly disappointed. Having served you for so long, could you not have fulfilled her last desire atleast? Is this the reward for your loyal service?" I told them tersely, "She did not die. You keep quiet." They could not believe My words. They queried "How do you presume that she did not die? The ants are crawling all over her body. There is no life in her body. Is it not true?" But, I silenced them saying, "I gave a word to her that I would pour a few drops of water in her mouth at the time of her leaving the body. I will never go back on My word." Subbamma's mother was a centenarian. I told her to bring some water dipping a few leaves of Tulasi (basil plant) in it. I went near the body of Subbamma and removed the cloth covering the body. I called her "Subbamma! Subbamma!" She opened her eyes slowly and held My hands tightly. She shed tears of joy and gratitude. Everyone witnessing that scene was wonder-struck. They shouted in one voice "Subbamma came back to life!" That was in fact, not true. What had actually happened was Subbamma came back to life only for My sake, since I gave a word to her and that had to be fulfilled. That is why she came back to life, momentarily. She enquired "Swami! when did you come?" I replied "Subbamma! I came just now". Thus, when she opened her eyes and started talking to Swami, all her relatives hurriedly went inside the house to make arrangements for Swami's stay and lunch. But, I told them firmly "You need not make any preparations for My food. I have come to see Subbamma. I saw her. Now, I will go straight to Puttaparthi." I held the hand of Subbamma and enquired her "What are you thinking about?" she replied "I am chanting Sairam! Sairam! Sairam! Swami". She shed tears of joy. I wiped her tears with My handkerchief. Holding My hand with great joy she expressed her feelings thus: "Swami! How nice of you to have come all the way to fulfil your promise made to me long ago! Do you still remember that promise, Swami! How compassionate you are!" Sathya Sai is not the type of person who goes back on his word. His very name is Sathyam. What he speaks and acts upon is also Sathyam (Truth).

In the meanwhile, Subbamma's mother, younger brothers, sisters and the Doctors-all people came in. They thought "How is it that Subbamma is talking all the while? How is it possible? There is no breathing in her body since last night! What a wonder! May be, this is Sai Baba's miracle!" Subbamma held My hand and put it on her forehead. Then, I created some vibhuthi and applied it on her forehead. I told her, "Subbamma! whatever worry you had till now is removed. Is it not? you were worried that Swami was not by your side in your last moments. Now you have seen Swami and heard his words. You have also held his hand. I am now going to Puttparthi. You close your eyes peacefully." She said "Thank you, Swami! Thank you! You go to Puttaparthi after sending me to my final abode." I told her "Now you close your eyes peacefully." I then poured a few drops of Tulasi water in her mouth. Thus, I kept up My promise. She put her both hands on My feet. I bade goobye to her saying "Subbamma! I fulfilled My promise made to you. Now you can go happliy." Subbamma then left her mortal coil saying "What more do I require Swami! I am leaving the body happily. Sairam! Sairam!" All the while, she was shedding tears of joy, holding My hands. Thus, she attained salvation. Once I give a word to someone, I will never forget. I will always abide by My word. Several people cannot believe this Truth. They think "Ah! Swami is saying something just casually." My word will never go waste. Whatever I say, I will act accordingly. This is the Truth.

The dead body of Subbamma was taken to the burial ground. It was placed on the funeral pyre and her younger brother lit the pyre. Strangely, her face remained serene till her entire body was consigned to the flames. That created a sensation in the village and became the talk of the village. I started on My return journey from Bukkapatnam to Puttaparthi, for which a bullock cart was kept ready. The brother of Griham Ammayi (Easwaramma), Chandramouli was with Me in the bullock cart. We saw smoke emanating from the cremation ground, where Subbamma's mortal remains were being consigned to flames. Chandramouli then asked Me "Swami! you were by the side of Subbamma's dead body till now. Why did you not wait till the cremation was over?" I told him "Chandramouli! I am not a person who goes back on his word. I gave a word to Subbamma that I would be present by her side during her last moments and pour water into her mouth. That I fulfilled. I blessed her to depart from this world peacefully. I kept My promise and came out." Chandramouli felt very happy and commented "Swami! How compassionate you are towards the devotees! In fact, words fail to describe your compassion." True! words fail to describe Swami's love and compassion towards Subbamma! Similarly, the devotion and surrender of Subbamma towards Swami are indescribable. Her devotion surpassed even that of Prahlada.

People had by now come to know about the news that Swami had fulfilled the promise given by Him to Subbamma and brought her back to life and poured water in her mouth during her last moments. The very next day, people came in large numbers in cars, one after the other. They started talking among themselves "It seems Subbamma was brought back to life by Swami. It seems Sai Baba poured water into her mouth during her last moments." The entire house of Subbamma was filled with these people. Everyone present there praised the good fortune of Subbamma. There was only one word on the lips of everybody "Sai Baba filfilled His promise. Subbamma's life has become sanctified." From that day onwards, several elderly people started visiting Me with a request "Swami! Please give a word to us also. You must pour sanctified water into our mouths at the time of our departure from this world." However, I used to tell them "My dear ones! All people cannot get this great boon. It you are destined to get it, you will certainly get it. I will come at the appropriate moment and pour sanctified water into your mouth."

16

Kondama Raju Departs

KONDAMA Raju, the grandfather of this body used to come all the way from the village to the Prasanthi Mandir by walk every morning and evening to have My *darshan*. One day I asked him "Why do you take so much trouble to come here and get back everyday twice? You remain in your own place. I will Myself come there to see you." Kondamaraju felt a little embarassed. He said "Ayyo Swami! Is it proper on my part to make you visit Me?" Clapping his cheeks apologetically, he continued "No, No, Swami! I will myself come to the Mandir to have Swami's *darshan*. This will be a good exercise for me." He also said "I am repeating your own words told to me earlier." (He was referring to Swami's reply to him when he proposed that Swami may take lunch in the Bukkapatnam school itself, instead of rushing to Puttaparthi and again getting back during the lunch hour). He was by then 112 years old. Even in that advanced age, he had his eyes, ears, legs and hands in good condition. He was able to come by walk from the Old Mandir to the New Mandir, even without the support of a walking stick. I used to warn him "there may be cattle coming in your way. Why don't you bring one stick alongwith you?" He used to reply "Why do I need a stick Swami? My God-given legs are in good conditon." He had great devotion towards Swami. He used to say "Swami! you are God, verily. No one except you and I know this truth."

I used to take pan regularly in those days. Right from early morning till I went to bed, I used to chew betel leaves and nut, with a little lime added to it. He also had the same habit. One day, I informed him "I put the betel leaves, nut powder and lime there." He protested "Swami! why do I need powdered nut? I am not an old person." So saying, he took the betel leaves and nuts and chewed them making good sound. His teeth were so strong even in that advanced age. His vision was in good condition. He could walk with ease, any distance. The old people in those days used to be so strong. What could be the reason? They used to make proper use of their body and senses. They used to live with a purpose "I must perform my duty, having been born as a human being."

Kondama Raju used to come to the Prasanthi Mandir, early in the morning. I used to sleep on the sand in front of the Mandir. Since I knew that he was coming to have My *darshan*, I used to cover Myself with a bed sheet fully covering My face also. That was to ensure that he does not know I was awake. He used to slowly lift the bed sheet over My feet, perform *Padanamaskar* (prostrations to My feet) and silently leave that place. He used to feel a little embarassment on such occassions that if anybody sees him then, they may think that this elderly gentleman of ripe old age is prostrating before his grandson, who is very young. Every human being is prone to such feeling, because of which he may not be able to express himself properly. The moment he left, I used to get up.

"One can wake up a person fast asleep,
How can one wake up the one that pretends to sleep?
Why delay Oh! Krishna! Enough, enough of your pranks."

(Telugu poem)

So sang the gopikas about Lord Krishna, in the *Dwapara yuga*.

Once, Kondamaraju asked Me "Swami! How long do I live? when do I leave this body?" I told him that I would give him My *darshan* before he departs from this world. He was a good singer. If he starts singing about the incident of Lakshmana falling unconscious in the Rama-Ravana war, the entire village used to flock round him. One evening, I went into the village of Puttaparthi. He was, at that time, sitting on a cot and singing some songs. When I reached that place, he immediately got down from the cot and fell on My feet exclaiming "Swami! you came!", unable to control his joy. He pleaded with Me "Swami! you are not an ordinary child. I know you are Lord Easwara, verily. You have taken birth in our lineage in order to help us cross the ocean of *samsara*. I have a small desire. Wayback in *Tretha Yuga*, King Dasaratha desired to leave his mortal coil after drinking a few drops of sanctified water from the hands of Srirama. But, he could not get his wish fulfilled. On the other hand, it was Jatayu, the bird who fought with Ravana when he was abducting Sita that could get this *prapthi* (blessing). I sincerely, pray to you to kindly shower such a blessing on Me also. Before I leave this body, you must power a few drops of water into my mouth with your divine hands." I gave him word that it shall happen accordingly.

Kondama Raju had a great liking for *'obbatlu'* (a kind of pancake). On the day before he died, he requested Easwaramma, his daughter-in-law to prepare them. Accordingly, she prepared some *obbatlu* and gave Me also a few of them. I told her "I will not partake sweets".

Kondama Raju insisted that I partake atleast one *obbattu*. He prayed "Swami! My end is nearing. This body is 112 years' old. Before I leave this body, I must put a piece of this preparation in your mouth with My own hands. People say Yasoda fed child Krishna with her own hands, Kausalya fed child Rama with her own hands, etc. Today, I think I have such good fortune. Hence, please permit Me to put a piece of this sweetmeat in your mouth with My hands. He, infact, put one piece. And lo! Surprisingly, it was neither in My mouth nor in his hands! Easwaramma, who was observing this scene, enquired Kondama Raju "Oh! Father-in-law! where did you loose that piece of *obbatlu*?" He replied "Can any one describe fully the divine pranks of Swami? They are not one or two. They are infinite."

I used to have a 'Morris Tourer' small car in those days, which I was driving Myself. I used to go around in that car, not only in this village but to far off places like Madras. When I was driving that car with great speed, people standing on the road side used to wonder at My speed. One day Kondama Raju called Easwaramma and said "See whether Swami is coming towards Sathyabhama Temple" Easwaramma came out and saw and confirmed "Yes; Swami is coming in His Car." Kondama Raju then told her "Easwaramma! My end is nearing. I will be no more. That is why God is coming here to keep up His word." Poor lady!

Easwaramma enquired innocently in the worldly sense "What! Father-in-law! Where is God? How does He come?" Kondama Raju then pointed towards Me and said "you innocent woman! Are you under the illusion that 'Sathya' is still your own son? Look! God is coming". Easwaramma also knew about My Divinity. She also witnessed the super-human powers of Swami, several times. Yet, she was deluded to think that I was her young 'sathya', out of her motherly love. Yasoda also used to be like that. Inspite of witnessing the fourteen *Lokas* (worlds) in the mouth of Krishna, she wondered whether it was "a dream or an illusion created by Lord Vishnu."

Kondama Raju then called Easwaramma and said "Easwaramma! God Himself is coming to take me away with Him. He is coming here to keep up His word given to me long ago. Please bring some water in a tumbler. He will pour a few drops in My mouth. Then, I will depart from this world peacefully". Easwaramma enquired "You don't have fever or any other disease. You are hale and healthy. How do you say you will die peacefully?" Kondama Raju replied "Death knows no reason or season. It will happen according to God's will. Therefore, please bring some water." Easwaramma then brought some water in a tumbler as requested by him, since she did not like to enter into an argument with him over the issue. Kondama Raju asked her to put a basil leaf in that water. He knew fully well that Swami was coming there only "to see him off." That was a fact known only to two people-Swami and himself.

He was waiting for My arrival, holding the tumbler in his hand. As soon as I arrived there, he said "Swami! I am ready." I told him "I am also ready." Kondama Raju sat down on the floor and asked Me to sit on the cot. He put his head on My knees and prayed "Swami! I have a submission. Kindly listen." Easwaramma was listening to our conversation. She was wondering "What a strange sight! How this elderly gentleman is giving so much respect to his young grandson!" But, she kept her thoughts to herself. Kondama Raju expressed his feelings thus: "Swami! you came here today to fulfill your promise given to Me some twenty years ago. The sky may break and fall down. The seas may go dry. But, your promise will never go waste." I just smiled at his words. He then requested Me "Swami! Please do not divert my thoughts with your enchanting smile. Take this glass and drink a portion of the water therein and pour the balanace quantity in my mouth with your divine hands." He also said "King Dasaratha had four sons after performing the *Puthrakamesti Yaga* (a sacrificial ritual performed with a desire to beget a son). Lord Narayana himself was born to him as Sri Rama and Aadisesha (The serpent upon whose coils Lord Narayana reclined) as Lakshmana and His conch and wheel as Bharatha and Sathrughna. Inspite of begetting such great sons, none of them was available by the side of king Dasaratha to pour a few drops of water in his mouth, during his last moments. Swami! you are born in our Rathnakara lineage. It is our great fortune that the Lord Himself took birth in our lineage with the Bharadwaja Gothra and Aapasthamba Suthra. Please, therefore, fulfil my last request. Let me not die with disappointment like that Dasaratha." He prayed thus. I told him "I came here exactly for that purpose." So saying, I lifted the tumbler and was about to pour the water contained therein, in Kondama Raju's mouth. He protested "No, No, Swami! you please drink the water first and then pour the remaining quantity in my mouth." Accordingly, I drank a little water from the tumbler and thereafter poured the balance in his mouth. Kondama Raju felt immensely happy and contented. He could not contain his feelings. He expressed "Swami! What a great fortune it is to drink water from your divine hands and then leave the mortal coil! Not all people can get this great fortune. Even a person of the stature of King Dasaratha could not get this unique opportunity. But, I could get it, I am so fortunate. My life has become sanctified." Expressing his feelings thus, he breathed his last with an everlasting smile on his face. Thus, all the members of that family died peacefully and effortlessly. Their lives are a perfect example for the adage that good begets good. Because of their noble feelings, everything in their life went on smoothly and ultimately they attained a noble and sacred end. I would advise that you may also constantly contemplate upon God till your last breath, in keeping with the saying *"Sarvada Sarvakaleshu Sarvathra Hari chinthanam"* (Everywhere, at all times and under all circumstances contemplate on God). When you do this, you will also attain a noble end, when time comes.

Kondama Raju used to run a small pan shop, where sundry articles like beedies (country cigars) betel leaves and nuts were being sold. Before he died, one day he called on Me and gave Me some money and requested "Swami! I never did any injustice to anybody nor did I ever deceive anybody. But, it is possible that I might have forgotten to return an anna or a paisa to somebody, by mistake. Since you have chosen to incarnate in our Ratnakara lineage, our entire lineage is sanctified. I do not want to die in debt to someone. Please, therefore, arrange to convert this money into small coins and scatter it on my dead body during my funeral procession. By so doing, I will be redeemed of any debt that may still be remaining." I told him "why should you have to give Me money for that purpose? I can get it done with the money available with Me." But, he insisted "No; Swami! My debt has to be cleared with My own money." Thus, all the members of that family were men of great sacrifice. It is only because of their virtue of sacrifice, they could win the grace of God. God's grace is the only wealth that a man should aspire for. If only that grace is available, everything else would automatically follow.

17

"I Myself Selected My Parents"

BEFORE he left his mortal coil, Kondama Raju gave a piece of advice to Easwaramma. He said "Easwaramma! The glory of Swami will spread to the entire world, in no time. In fact, the world itself will undergo a great change. People of several countries will come here. You don't get deluded by the feeling 'Swami is My boy, My son' and develop motherly attachment. Swami does not belong to this family, exclusively. You are still immersed in the illusory motherly relationship, based upon the physical body. All the relationships based upon the physical body are like the fleeting clouds. Only the *Atmic* relationship is eternal. Hence, reduce your attachment to the physical body. Cultivate attachment to the *Atma*." Advising thus, Kondama Raju put his hand on her head and blessed her. From that day onwards, Easwaramma started living in the Prasanthi Nilayam, leaving her house. She used to come to Swami's room everyday morning and evening and talk to Him. It is a fact that she also realised the divinity of Swami, well. Sometimes, when Swami appeared as Lord Easwara, she used to be a bit confused saying "Swami! what are all these serpents?" I used to pretend innocence saying "I did not wear any serpents round my neck!" Later, when she looked at Me carefully, she could not find any serpents over My body. Thus, she witnessed Swami's divinity directly, several times. Same is the case with Kausalya, the mother of Lord Sri Rama and Yasoda, the foster mother of Lord Sri Krishna. All these people used to live under an illusion, out of motherly affection. Divinity is shrouded thus, in mystery. Let Me reveal to you a small miracle happened in the present *Avathar*. After the Prasanthi Mandir was built, I used to take My meal in the room on the right side of the first floor. The Griham Ammayi (Easwaramma) used to come there during that time and pressurise Me to eat more, saying "Swami! you are not taking sufficient food and hence becoming thin. Please eat more." I used to reply "Do I have to fight with anybody? Do I have to become stout? No, No. I don't like becoming stout." One day, someone invited Me for lunch in their house. They wanted to kill Me, by mixing poison in the food. They were jealous of My reputation growing more and more day by day. By the time I returned from their house after taking food there, the colour of My body turned into blue and froth started coming out of My mouth. Then, I instructed Easwaramma to turn her hand in full circle. While she did so, vibhuthi appeared in her hands. She wondered "How come! I have seen *vibhuthi* appearing when Swami turns His hand in a circular motion. But, how did it appear in my hands!" In fact, it is I who granted that power to her for that short period. She then mixed the *vibhuthi* in a glass of water and gave it to Me to drink. The moment I drank that water mixed with the *vibhuthi*, the effect of the poison disappeared miraculously.

I Myself have selected the parents of this body. Pedda Venkama Raju used to help the devotees a lot. Whenever they wanted articles like coconuts or pulses, he used to go immediately to Bukkapatnam and get them. He did great service to the devotees. On the day of his departure from this world, he came to the Mandir to see Me. I had already selected some people for interview. As I was about to go into the interview room, he came and stood before the pillar. I asked him "On what purpose you came here?" He replied "I have a small work with you, Swami! I wish to talk to you for a minute." I told him "Wait, wait! I will call you after seeing these people." But, he was in a hurry and said "No, Swami! I must talk to you urgently." Thus, he prevailed upon Me.

Then I told him "O.K., come in." He used to keep all his money carefully wrapped in a piece of cloth and tuck it in his *dhothi* at the waist. In those days, there were no money purses. He took out all that money and placed it in My hands. He then requested Me "Swami! I do not want to die as a person indebted to somebody. I must be free from all sorts of debts. It is possible that I might have been indebted to someone to the extent of an anna or a quarter of an anna, during my business transactions. I, therefore, brought this money to redeem Myself of such debts. This is the money I have earned by the sweat of my brow." So saying, he handed over some money to Me. He also requested "Swami! I have also kept apart five bags of rice and some pulses. I have also kept two packets of jaggery. On the twelfth day after My death, please arrange for poor feeding with these provisions and money". He then went straight to his house from the Mandir and called "Who is there?" He was not in the habit of calling his wife by her name. Easwaramma came out and enquired "What do you want?". He asked her to fetch some water, drank it and breathed his last. He died so easily and peacefully. He did not suffer for a minute even. He came to Me, talked to Me, then went straight to his house by walk, lied down and breathed his last.

Easwaramma too died effortlessly in the same manner. The Summer classes were being held in

Sri Pedda Venkama Raju

Mother Easwaramma

Bangalore, then. She used to wish for the opportunity to be with Swami, wherever He went. Therefore, she also attended the summer course. She felt very happy to see the boys attending those classes. She used to supply drinking water to those children while they were taking food. In fact, she used to think gleefully "Is it not because of Swami that we had this good fortune!" One day, the children were being served breakfast as usual. She also had her breakfast and coffee. Venkamma always used to be with her, to attend to her needs. After finishing her breakfast, Easwaramma wanted to have her pan. She therefore started pounding the betel nuts with the help of a small mortar and pestle. I could hear that sound from My room situated in the first floor. Suddenly, she called Me "Swami! Swami!" I replied "I am coming, I am coming." She again called "Please come quickly." I came down and she breathed her last. She had no pain of any sort. She did not suffer for even a minute. Both the parents of this body left their mortal coil in the same manner, so effortlessly. Since Swami selected them to be His parents, their lives were so sacred and sanctified. Those who are pure and sacred will have a sacred end. This is true in the case of Kondama Raju, Peda Venkama Raju and Easwaramma also! They are all "selected people." Swami selected them. This is how the story of Swami went on. I did not cause even the slightest inconvenience to anyone. I did not talk harshly to anybody, lest they may feel hurt. If at all I wanted to scold anybody, I will just say *"Dunnapotha!"* (He-buffalo). That itself is a big reprimand, so far as I am concerned. More than this, I do not know any other word to reprimand someone. Eversince My childhood, I have been making everybody happy, without hurting them in any way.

Some *Avathars* had come as a result of the prayers of their parents. But, in this *Avathar*, it is I who decided that so and so shall be My father and mother and accordingly granted them birth as such. This body is not born in a normal way in the ordinary parents-son relationship. It is by an immaculate conception.

18

"The Lord Of Puttaparthi Will Protect You Always"

EASWARAMMA belonged to a very poor family. She never used to have a paisa in her hand. She is not known to have eaten rice anytime in her life. She always used to partake '*Ragi Sankati*' (ragi gruel). That had been My habit too! In fact, I like it most. Behind the success of every great man, there is his mother. The noble mothers, with their devotion and surrender, with their ritual worship and prayers have been continuously moulding the character and personality of their children, so that they blossom into great men and women in this country. They may not possess high education and academic degrees. But, their character and nobility is their strength. In fact, this village of Puttaparthi has acquired great name and fame only because of the noble qualities of Easwaramma, who did not have any formal education. Unfortunately, today people are extolling the son of Easwaramma, forgetting Easwaramma herself. From where did this great *Avathar* come, without Easwaramma? Hence, one should appreciate the role of the mother and protect the honour and glory of the mother. One should respect the Mother. The glory of Sri Sathya Sai has spread everywhere, in this fashion.

Very high officials used to come to Me, even in those days. The Griham Ammayi used to fear very much if someone with a police uniform appeared. Immediately she used to come home and request Subbamma "Subbamma! The police people might cause some inconvenience to Swami. Please do not allow them to come near Swami!" Subbamma used to allay her fears saying "They are also devotees. Everyone will come to Swami for His blessings. You need not fear them." Still Easwaramma was not to be convinced. She used to say "It is only because Swami is residing in your house, all the police people are coming." Once, the Inspector General of Police, Ranganaikulu came to take Me to Madras. Then, Griham Ammayi started crying, inconsolably! That was the first time I was going to Madras. In those days, the people of Puttaparthi used to believe that Madras was a distant foreign country!

Easwaramma heard the villagers talking among themselves; "They are taking Swami to some distant foreign country." She decided, "I will not allow them to take Swami alongwith them. I will obstruct them." She also cried before Me saying "Swami! you should not go, you should not go." Such was her motherly love and affection towards Swami. She was always under the apprehension that people may take Swami to some distant foreign lands.

Gradually, people from distant places like Bangalore used to come to Puttaparthi and pray that Swami may visit their places. Devotees like Coffee Estate Sakamma, the Maharani of Mysore and the maternal uncle of the Maharaja of Mysore used to come here in their cars. In those days, people coming to Puttaparthi by car had to park their cars in Karnata Nagepalli, a village on the eastern bank of the river Chitravathi, and come by walk wading through knee - deep water. Once they prayed "Swami! It is becoming very difficult for us to come to this remote village and get back. You please come and stay in Mysore. We will give you a lot of land there. We will also build an *Ashram* for you. But, I firmly refused their offer saying "I don't need your lands or *Ashrams*. This land of Puttaparthi is my land. Did you not hear the saying *'Janani Janmabhumischa Swargadapi Gariyasi'* (The mother and mother land are greater than even heaven). This village appears to be a tiny and remote village to you, at this juncture. But, in course of time, you will yourself observe how much this village will develop."

On another day, a devotee by name Sakamma prayed "Swami! It is becoming very difficult for us to come to this village and again get back to our places. There is no proper road even for our cars to come here. It is very difficult to come to this village even by a bullock cart. Please, therefore come away to Bangalore. We will build a palatial building there for you to stay." I told her " I don't need such big buildings. This small room here is enough for Me". Thus, she used to pressurize Me, inspite of My turning down her requests. Easwaramma came to Me that night with great tension and anxiety and requested "Swami! I am observing that a number of people from far-off places are coming here and requesting you to come to that place and this place. Their efforts are meant to take you away from here, for their selfish ends. I will not survive, if you leave Puttaparthi. Take for example, the case of a plant. It is only when a sapling is nourished and nurtured in the place in which it sprouted originally, it will grow into a huge tree. If you keep that plant in one place today and remove it and transplant it in a different place after sometime, how can it grow? Hence, you please stay permanently in the village in which you are born. You may go anywhere, but never leave Puttaparthi. You

Smt. Sakamma

Sri Venugopala Swami Temple

Prasanthi Nilayam, Nov. 1950

promise me that you will reside here only." Then, I gave a promise to her that I will never leave Puttaparthi, under any circumstances. I also told her. "I will stay here only. I will just visit My devotees and come back." Later on, a Mandir was built here, for which Easwaramma alone was responsible.

Since I made a promise to Easwaramma that day, I did not leave Puttaparthi till today. Whoever he may be, one has to come to this place only. The question of My staying elsewhere does not arise at all! Today, several people are leaving their native places. One should never leave his native place. That is the motto of this *Avathar*. If a tree that is grown in this place is uprooted and transplanted in a different place, how can it survive? This gigantic tree called 'Sai Baba' must grow in the same place where it was born. Since, I did not leave Puttaparthi and continued to stay here, this village has grown into a great spiritual centre for the entire world.

In fact, there is a strange history behind this village acquiring the name of Puttaparthi. There used to be a small snake-mound in the place where the Venugopala Swamy Temple is now situated. A snake used to live in that mound. The cow-herds of this village used to take their cows to the outskirts everyday for grazing. But, one of the cows used to somehow escape and go near the snake-mound. The snake in the mound used to come out and suck the milk direct from the udder of the cow, without causing any harm to it. One day, some of the cowherd boys observed this strange scene and tried to kill the snake. They picked up a big stone and threw it on the snake, while it was sucking milk from the udder of the cow. Then the snake cursed the villagers saying "Neither the cowherds nor the cows can survive in this village." It died soon after. That is the reason why the cowherds of Puttaparthi left their village and settled in a place a little away, called Gokulam. From that day onwards, the cowherds never used to sleep in the village of Puttaparthi. By evening, they used to return to Gokulam. The same stone which was thrown upon the snake and killed it that day is now being worshipped in the Venugopala Swami Temple.

I narrated all this story with a view to tell you the reason for spread of the glory of Sai Baba to the entire world today as also the reason behind this village acquiring the name of Puttaparthi. This Puttparthi has a great history behind it. This is not a name given to it just for fun's sake. Several great personalities and spiritual aspriants visited this place. Several noble souls resided in this village and strove to uphold the name and fame of Puttaparthi. The Maharaja of Mysore used to visit Puttaparthi, in those days. His mother was a noble and orthodox lady. She used to alight from her car at Karnata Nagepalli and walk all the way to reach this place. Thus, this village of Puttaparthi was venerated and held in high esteem by several great men and women. The population of Puttparthi in those days was a mere 150 people. Today, lakhs and lakhs of people are visiting this place. If you just have a look at it, you can observe how several sky-rise buildings have come up in this small village. All the people in this village have prospered. A big University, a Super-speciality Hospital and an Aerodrome that can not be found even in big cities have come up in this once remote village of Puttaparthi.

"The Lord of Puttaparthi will protect you always,
He is the Embodiment of Compassion;
He will hold your hand and take you across the ocean of Samsara,
He will never forsake you under any circumstances."
(Telugu poem)

What great things have been achieved by this Prasanthi Nilayam during the last fifty years are not possible even in five hundred years, normally. Eventhough a number of *Avathars* had come earlier, such great changes have not been achieved in a mere fifty years' time. All these works have been achieved single-handed. A big University has been started. A Planetarium has been built. An Aerodrome has come up in this small remote village of Puttaparthi. The glory of Prasanthi Nilayam has spread to the entire world. In fact, the entire world is now in Prasanthi Nilayam only. People of all the countries in the world are coming to Prasanthi

Nilayam. Prasanthi Nilayam itself has become a 'mini world'. You will witness the glory of Puttaparthi further, in the years to come. We are not inviting anyone to come here. We are not undertaking any propaganda about Prasanthi Nilayam. Will people come by invitation? In fact, I am telling people "don't come here, don't come here." Still, they are coming from all over the world in large numbers. It is only Divinity that will have such power of attraction. When a flower blossoms, its fragrance spreads everywhere. Does the flower invite the bumble - bee to come and suck its honey. No, No. It is only the bees that come buzzing from a long distance, rest on the flower and suck the honey contained in the flower. It is only because there is honey in the flowers that the bees come and rest on the flowers. Otherwise, do they perch on a plastic flower?

Embodiments of Love! you are really blessed souls. You are very fortunate. You have been able to spend time happily moving with Swami and singing and playing with him. You are with Sai and Sai is with you. That is why I have been telling you always "I and you are one." No one can describe the power of Divinity. He is omnipotent. His power is infinite. Hence, I would advise you to cultivate faith in God:

"Encircling which town the sacred river of
Chitravathi flows in all its pristine beauty;

Around which town there are beautiful mango groves
symbolising auspiciousness;
Standing guard on the four sides of which town are
the deities of Parvathi and Parameswara;
Firmly installed in the midst of which town is the
effulgent Lord Vishnu in all His splendour;
That world-famous town is Puttapuram or Puttaparthi
with its fresh water tank built by Chikkavadiyar;
Standing as an ever lasting monument to the glory of
Bukkaraya."

(Telugu poem)

SRI SATHYA SAI BOOKS AND PUBLICATIONS TRUST
PRASANTHI NILAYAM

PIN 515 134, ANANTAPUR DISTRICT, ANDHRA PRADESH, INDIA
IMPORTER / EXPORTER CODE NO. 0990001032
RESERVE BANK OF INDIA EXPORTER CODE NO. HS-2001198

THE VAHINI SERIES : (BOOKS WRITTEN BY BHAGAWAN SRI SATHYA SAI BABA)

	Price Rs.	Wt. in Gms. approx.
Bhagavatha Vahini (The story of the Glory of the Lord)	44.00	490
Dharma Vahini (Stream of Righteousness)	20.00	230
Dhyana Vahini (Stream of Meditation)	20.00	210
Geetha Vahini (The Divine Gospel)	32.00	415
Jnana Vahini (The Stream of Eternal Wisdom)	16.00	165
Leela Kaivalya Vahini (The Cosmic Play of God)	9.00	75
Prasanthi Vahini (The Supreme Bliss of Divine)	15.00	140
Prasnottara Vahini (Answers to Spiritual Questions)	15.00	95
Prema Vahini (The Stream of Divine Love)	20.00	125
Rama Katha Rasa Vahini Part-I (The Sweet Story of Rama's Glory)	48.00	705
Rama Katha Rasa Vahini Part-II (The Sweet Story of Rama's Glory)	36.00	460
Sandeha Nivarini (Clearance of Spiritual Doubts)	18.00	230
Sathya Sai Vahini (Spiritual Message of Sri Sathya Sai)	34.00	406
Sutra Vahini (Stream of Aphorisms on Brahman)	19.00	110
Upanishad Vahini (Essence of Vedic Knowledge)	18.00	225
Vidya Vahini (Flow of Spiritual Education)	17.00	210

SATHYA SAI SPEAKS SERIES:
(DISCOURSES BY BHAGAWAN SRI SATHYA SAI BABA) (REVISED & ENLARGED EDITIONS)

	Price Rs.	Wt. in Gms. approx.
Sathya Sai Speaks Vol. I (Years 1953 to 1960)	34.00	390
Sathya Sai Speaks Vol. II (Years 1961 to 1962)	39.00	490
Sathya Sai Speaks Vol. III (Year 1963)	38.00	420
Sathya Sai Speaks Vol. IV (Year 1964)	39.00	510
Sathya Sai Speaks Vol. V (Year 1965)	43.00	535
Sathya Sai Speaks Vol. VI (Year 1966)	59.00	465
Sathya Sai Speaks Vol. VII (Year 1967)	40.00	410
Sathya Sai Speaks Vol. VIII (Year 1968)	39.00	425
Sathya Sai Speaks Vol. IX (Year 1969)	30.00	345
Sathya Sai Speaks Vol. X (Year 1970)	35.00	450
Sathya Sai Speaks Vol. XI (Years 1971 to 1972)	45.00	565
Sathya Sai Speaks Vol. XII (Years 1973 to 1974)	42.00	535
Sathya Sai Speaks Vol. XIII (Years 1975 to 1977)	30.00	445
Sathya Sai Speaks Vol. XIV (Years 1978 to 1979) (Part I)	30.00	–
Sathya Sai Speaks Vol. XIV (Years 1979 to 1980) (Part II)	34.00	–
Sathya Sai Speaks Vol. XV (Years 1981 to 1982)	40.00	550
Sathya Sai Speaks Vol.XVI (Year 1983)	30.00	330
Sathya Sai Speaks Vol. XVII (Year 1984)	32.00	–
Sathya Sai Speaks Vol. XVIII (Year 1985)	25.00	365
Sathya Sai Speaks Vol. XIX (Year 1986)	30.00	405
Sathya Sai Speaks Vol. XX (Year 1987)	39.00	460
Sathya Sai Speaks Vol. XXI (Year 1988)	35.00	455
Sathya Sai Speaks Vol. XXII (Year 1989)	35.00	475
Sathya Sai Speaks Vol. XXIII (Year 1990)	44.00	510
Sathya Sai Speaks Vol. XXIV (Year 1991)	40.00	540
Sathya Sai Speaks Vol. XXV (Year 1992)	40.00	645
Sathya Sai Speaks Vol. XXVI (Year 1993)	50.00	655
Sathya Sai Speaks Vol. XXVII (Year 1994)	35.00	510
Sathya Sai Speaks Vol. XXVIII (Year 1995)	43.00	620
Sathya Sai Speaks Vol. XXIX (Year 1996)	43.00	635
Sathya Sai Speaks Vol. XXX (Year 1997)	35.00	490
Sathya Sai Speaks Vol. XXXI (Year 1998)	53.00	730
Sathya Sai Speaks Vol. XXXII (Year 1999) - Part 1	27.00	370
Sathya Sai Speaks Vol. XXXII (Year 1999) - Part 2	27.00	370
Sathya Sai Speaks Vol. XXXIII (Year 2000)	39.00	495
Sathya Sai Speaks Vol. XXXIV (Year 2001)	38.00	462
Sathya Sai Speaks Vol.XXXV (Year 2002)	40.00	525
Sathya Sai Speaks Vol.XXXVI (Year 2003) - Part - 1	29.00	330

	Price Rs.	Wt. in Gms. approx.
Sathya Sai Speaks Vol.XXXVI (Year 2003) - Part - 2	23.00	250
Sathya Sai Speaks Vol.XXXVII (Year 2004)	38.00	400
Sathya Sai Speaks Vol.XXXVIII (Year 2005)	29.00	–
SATHYAM SIVAM SUNDARAM SERIES: (LIFE STORY OF BHAGAVAN SRI SATHYA SAI BABA)		
Sathyam Sivam Sundaram Vol. 1 (Birth to 1961)	60.00	595
Sathyam Sivam Sundaram Vol. 2 (1962 to 1968)	49.00	515
Sathyam Sivam Sundaram Vol. 3 (1969 to 1972)	48.00	425
Sathyam Sivam Sundaram Vol. 4 (1973 to 1979)	40.00	430
Sathyam Sivam Sundaram Vol. 5 (1980 to 1985)	55.00	605
Sathyam Sivam Sundaram Vol. 1 to 5 (Deluxe Edition)	390.00	–
SUMMER SHOWER SERIES : (DISCOURSES ON INDIAN CULTURE AND SPIRITUALITY BY BHAGAVAN SRI SATHYA SAI BABA)		
Summer Showers in Brindavan 1972	15.50	230
Summer Showers in Brindavan 1973 (New Enlarged Edition)	46.00	789
Summer Showers in Brindavan 1974 Part - I (New Enlarged Edition)	36.00	360
Summer Showers in Brindavan 1974 Part - II (New Enlarged Edition)	38.00	380
Summer Roses on the Blue Mountains (Ooty) 1976 (New Enlarged Edition)	34.00	360
Summer Showers in Brindavan 1977	17.50	175
Summer Showers in Brindavan 1978	46.00	510
Summer Showers in Brindavan 1979 (New Enlarged Edition)	34.00	325
Summer Showers in Brindavan 1990	25.00	275
Summer Showers in Brindavan 1991	22.00	285
Summer Showers in Brindavan 1993	23.00	200
Summer Showers in Brindavan 1995	34.00	280
Summer Showers in Brindavan 1996	19.00	205
Summer Showers in Brindavan 2000	34.00	460
Summer Showers in Brindavan 2002	25.00	300
CHILDREN'S BOOKS:		
Chinna Katha-Part I	30.00	350
Chinna Katha-Part II	42.00	385
Chinna Katha Illustrated	17.00	80
Chinna Katha Picture Stories Vol - 1	25.00	205
Chinna Katha Picture Stories Vol - 2	25.00	205
Chinna Katha Picture Stories Vol - 3	25.00	205
My Life is My Message	17.00	115
Stories for Children : Part I	17.00	190
Stories for Children : Part II	28.00	325
Divine Stories Vol 1 (Human Value Stories)	35.00	430
Divine Stories Vol 2 (Human Value Stories)	30.00	375
Ramakatha Rasavahini Pictorial - Vol. 1 - Purnima Ray	27.00	115
Ramakatha Rasavahini Pictorial - Vol. 2 - Purnima Ray	31.00	145
Ramakatha Rasavahini Pictorial - Vol. 3 - Purnima Ray	32.00	155
OUR OTHER PUBLICATIONS:		
Baba - The Breath of Sai by Grace J. Mc Martin	46.00	485
Bhagavan Uvacha Series Vol - 1	70.00	540
Bhagavan Uvacha Series Vol - 2	70.00	450
Bhagavad Gita (Part - I and II)	69.00	820
Birthday Blessings of Bhagavan	25.00	325
Be Like Jesus	32.00	320
Grama Seva is Rama Seva	20.00	255
Conversation with Bhagavan Sri Sathya Sai Baba by Dr. John S. Hislop	29.00	375
Fundamentals of Sri Sathya Sai Educare Vol. I - Compiled by Ranvir Singh	60.00	520
Fundamentals of Sri Sathya Sai Educare Vol. II - Compiled by Ranvir Singh	59.00	510
Fundamentals of Sri Sathya Sai Educare Vol. III - Compiled by Ranvir Singh	59.00	625
Fundamentals of Sri Sathya Sai Educare Vol. IV - Compiled by Ranvir Singh	64.00	625
Finding God by Charles Penn	50.00	705
Food for Thought	40.00	465
Gems of Wisdom	53.00	690
Guidelines to Active workers of S.S.S.S. Organisations from Bhagawan Baba	19.00	195
His story as told by Himself	29.00	300
Ati Rudra Maha Yajna (August 2006)	15.00	125
A Recapitulation of Baba's Divine Teachings by Grace J. Mc Martin	35.00	485

A pioneering attempt at child labour elimination - A tribute to Sai Baba, The Ultimate Motivator	35.00	335
Seva: A Flower At His Lotus Feet - Grace J. Mc Martin	29.00	325
Spirituality and Health by Dr. (Mrs) Charanjit Ghooi	60.00	725
Bhakthi and Health by Dr. (Mrs) Charanjit Ghooi	30.00	270
Benedictory Addresses (21 Convocation Discourses by Bhagavan as Chancellor from beginning up to 2002)	26.00	350
Easwaramma The Chosen Mother (Enlarged edition)	24.00	285
End of the Endless Search by P.P. Arya	28.00	265
Sathya Sai Education in Human Values	25.00	280
Garland of 108 Precious Gems (108 Holy Names of Bhagavan)	20.00	170
Journey to God - Part II - J. Jagadeesan	86.00	645
Loving God - N. Kasturi	52.00	725
Love of Conscience - Rita Bruce	26.00	305
Life is a Game Play It - Joy Thomas	42.00	465
Life is a Challenge Meet It - Joy Thomas	26.00	330
Life is Love Enjoy It - Joy Thomas	28.00	345
Life is a Dream Realise It - Joy Thomas	32.00	335
My Baba and I - Dr. John S. Hislop	42.00	455
My Beloved - Charles Penn	35.00	395
Nama Mahima	13.00	160
Namasmarana	8.00	55
Ocean of Love	500.00	1865
One Single Stream of Love	41.00	210
Pathway to Peace Prasanthi	21.00	235
Purifying the Heart - John Goldthwait, Ph.D	20.00	215
A Practice for Purifying the Heart - John Goldthwait, Ph.D	9.00	75
Rays of Radiance - Service Adoration Illumination - Prof. K. Anil Kumar	37.00	440
Sai Sandesh - Prof. K. Anil Kumar	48.00	275
Universal and Practical Teachings of Bhagavan - Prof. K. Anil Kumar	24.00	305
Sadhana - The Inward Path	41.00	475
Sai Baba - The Ultimate Experience - Phyllis Krystal	35.00	435
Sai Baba - The Holy Man and Psychiatrist - Dr. Samuel H. Sandweiss	58.00	440
Spirit and the Mind - Dr. Samuel H. Sandweiss	46.00	545
Sai Bhajanamala	45.00	570
Sai Baba's Mahavakya on Leadership (Hard Bound) - Lieut Gen. (Retd) Dr. M.L. Chibber	52.00	460
Sai Advent - Compiled by Harendra Singh	11.00	85
Sai Study Circle Manual	20.00	210
Sri Sathya Sai Gita – All about Spirituality in Qs & As - P.P. Arya	45.00	485
The Essential Sai	39.00	–
The Glory of Womanhood	17.00	205
To my Father - Justice Padma Kastgir	24.00	165
Sai Echoes from Kodai Hills	20.00	235
Quiz on Bhagavatam	10.00	50
Quiz on Mahaabhaaratha	7.00	50
Quiz on Raamaayana	7.00	50
Quiz on the Bhagavath Geeta	7.00	35
Quiz on Divine Life of Bhagavan Sri Sathya Sai Baba	6.00	65
Raso Vai Sah - Brahmananda Panda	48.00	450
Sai Baba and You - Practical Spirituality - Mark and Barbara Gardner	27.00	295
Seeking Divinity - Dr. John S. Hislop	32.00	385
Thought for the Day	26.00	215
Divine Discourses on Easwaramma Day	18.00	225
Divine Memories - Diana Baskin	47.00	485
Unforgettable Baba - Joyce Darlene Barker	40.00	335
Aura of the Divine	37.00	435
Sree Gurucharanam (A Compilation of Guru Poornima Discourses)	11.00	145
Prema Dhaara Vol. 1 (Letters written by Bhagavan to His students)	16.00	130
Prema Dhaara Vol. 2 (Letters / Messages from Bhagawan to His students / teachers and others)	29.00	325
The Light of Love	18.00	225
The Wish-Fulfilling Tree - Don Mario Mazzoleni	44.00	545
The Mind and its Mysteries	16.00	170
Truth is Only One	32.00	370
Prasanthi Nilayam Information Booklet	10.00	110
The Dharmic Challenge	25.00	335
The Direct Flight to Divinity	22.00	230

Dasara Discourses 1997 (Senses for Selfless Service)	15.00	160
Dasara Discourses 1998	19.00	200
Dasara Discourses 1999 & 2000	25.00	280
Dasara Discourses 2001	18.00	220
Dasara Discourses 2002	13.00	160
Dasara Discourses 2004	6.00	150
Dasara Discourses 2005	9.00	110
Message of the Lord	185.00	1575
Sathya Sai Parenting - Rita Bruce	33.00	390
Sri Sathya Sai Anandadayi - Karunamba Ramamurthy	48.00	550
Sri Sathya Sai Ved Vani - A compilation of discourses by Bhagavan Sri Sathya Sai Baba on Veda	50.00	560
Siva Sakthi Swarupa	13.00	130
The Mission of Sathya Sai at a Glance	70.00	430
Tribute	70.00	760
Vision of Sai I	47.00	465
Vision of Sai II	48.00	465
Who is a devotee of the Lord	12.00	85

FOR SALE ONLY IN INDIA

Transformation of the Heart - Judy Warner	28.00	285
Reconnecting the Love Energy - Phyllis Krystal	25.00	265
Taming our Monkey Mind - Phyllis Krystal	28.00	340
Suggestions for Study Groups and Individuals use of the Ceiling on Desires Programme	6.00	75
A Catholic Priest Meets Sai Baba - Don Mario Mazzoleni	34.00	490
Pathways to God Vol. I - Jonathan Roof	26.00	360
Pathways to God Vol. II - Jonathan Roof	39.00	385
Pathways to God Vol. III - Jonathan Roof	45.00	460
With Love Man is God - Samuel H. Sandweiss	115.00	755

Rates indicated are the prevailing rates. They are liable to change.

INLAND/OVERSEAS BOOK ORDERS

Books are despatched by Regd. Book Post only subject to availability. Indents and remittances within India should be received by Money Order/Indian Postal Order/Account Payee Cheques/Bank Drafts.

REMITTANCES

Remittances from Overseas towards Book Orders can be sent by A/C payee Bank Cheque / Demand Draft / International Money Order in **FOREIGN CURRENCY ONLY AND NOT IN INDIAN RUPEES.** Sending Cash Currency is liable to be confiscated by Government.

All remittances should be in favour of **THE CONVENER, SRI SATHYA SAI BOOKS AND PUBLICATIONS TRUST, PRASANTHI NILAYAM, ANANTAPUR DISTRICT, ANDHRA PRADESH, INDIA, PIN CODE-515 134,** payable at State Bank of India, Prasanthi Nilayam (Branch Code No. 2786) mentioning full address in capitals with Area Pin Code, Zip Code No., where the books are to be despatched.

The approximate postage + packing + forwarding charges for Overseas Sea Mail and Inland per packet are indicated below:

Wt. of Packets	Overseas		Inland
	APPU Countries	Others	
Up to 500 gms.	Rs.78/-	Rs.82/-	Rs.37/-
Above 500 gms. - Below 1 kg	Rs.93/-	Rs.100/-	Rs.42/-
Above 1 kg - Below 2 kg	Rs.109/-	Rs.118/-	Rs.52/-
Above 2 kg - Below 3 kg	Rs.135/-	Rs.150/-	Rs.72/-
Above 3 kg - Below 4 kg	Rs.162/-	Rs.180/-	Rs.82/-
Above 4 kg - Below 5 kg	Rs.188/-	Rs.212/-	Rs.92/-

N.B. Maximum weight allowed per packet is 5 kgs. Weight of packing materials *per packet* to be added to the weight of books – Overseas – 300 gms.

Inland up to 2 kgs – 100 gms. Above 2 kgs and up to 5 kgs – 300 gms.

APPU Countries: Afghanistan, Australia, Brunei, Cambodia, China (People's Republic), Fiji, Indonesia, Iran, Japan, Korea (Rep.), Laos (Rep.) Malaysia, Maldives, Myanmar, Naura, Papua New Guinea, Philippines, Solomon Island, Sri Lanka, Thailand, Vietnam, New Zealand, Singapore.